NAVIGATING THE JOURNEY

Our Journey to and Beyond the
Cathedral of the Holy Spirit

Kirby and Sandra Clements

CLEMENTS
MINISTRIES

Decatur, GA

Navigating the Journey: Our Journey to and Beyond the Cathedral of the Holy Spirit
Copyright 2014 Kirby and Sandra Clements

Address inquiries to the publisher:

Clements Family Ministry
2000 Cathedral Place
Decatur, Georgia 30034 USA

Learn more about the authors and their ministry at
www.clementsministries.org

ISBN: 978-0-9794181-4-3
LCCN: 2014955983

First Printing: November 2014
Printed in the United States of America

Editors: Merlene J. Purkiss, Annette Johnson, Anyce Stone

Dedication

To the memory of the Cathedral of the Holy Spirit

Preface

For almost 30 years, I was privileged to work very closely alongside Archbishop Earl Paulk, one of the most gifted churchmen in this century. He had a presbytery of some of the most dedicated and gifted ministers and a committed congregation comprised of many different races, cultures, and nationalities. This ministry was used to provoke a revival interest in the Kingdom of God, worship, unity, evangelism, local church, episcopacy, racial and denominational reconciliation and restoration of those who were estranged and fallen. From the beginning of my involvement in 1980, I have watched, listened, and learned from some of the most effective servants of the Lord, including our own local presbytery of men and women. Others who have visited and ministered among us included such names as TL and Daisy Osborn, LaDonna Osborn, Mel Bailey, Kelly Varner, John Avanzini, Jamie Buckingham, Emmanuel Cannestraci, Benson Idahosa, Margaret Idahosa, Iverna Thompkins, Harry Mushegan, Judson Cornwall, Oral Roberts, Dennis Peacock, Moses Vegh, Mark Hanby, Dave Demola, Viola Kitley, Mark Vehi, David Huskins, Charles Simpson, Ern Baxter, Bill Hamon, Daniel Juster, Don Meares, Robert McAlister, Gary North, Paul Paino, Carlton Pearson, Richard Roberts, Robert Schuller, Tom Skinner, Malcolm Smith, John Garlington, Joseph Garlington, Tom Hodgin, Tommie Reid, John Meares, and Andrew Young. My wife and I have also witnessed redeemed people desperately seeking to hear from God and obey. And we have also observed the consequences of human weaknesses and failures.

Since 1990, I have kept a diary of teachings and notes, impressions gleaned during times of prayer and study of the Word, and observations of the times, seasons and progressions of this ministry. These personal reflections and memories were never intended to be shared with anyone except my wife and children. Nevertheless, they revealed my observations of the power, character and ways of the Lord as expressed in judgments, choices, and decisions. After these many years, I have sensed the release to reveal my personal notes and observations. I must admit my joy, pain and even the revival of some disappointment in writing of this work. There are some memories that will never fade nor be wasted. There are also some prophecies, predictions and decrees that shall not be forgotten. There remains some controversies in my mind over what could or should have been and whether true repentance could have caused a fruitful tree to be cut down and spring up. There are faces and voices that I will never see nor hear again. Interestingly enough, during the writing of this work, my family and I reside in a home located directly 100 yards across from the old Cathedral building. In fact, we leave our home each day and drive directly past the old building. There is no worship of the elaborate physical structures, but 30 years of our lives were wonderfully spent worshiping the Lord on these grounds.

If there were any significant discovery or central theme, it would simply be that *His ways and thoughts are higher than ours* (Isaiah 55:8-9). Along this journey, we have also learned that only the Lord has the power to make promises and keep them. The only guarantee that people can provide is that they will always be human.

Admittedly, this is a God story and not a record of human

mistakes and failures. For this reason, names have been omitted except for the authors and the occasional mentioning of the founders. To allow the notoriety of the scandals to eclipse the legacy of this work would be a tragedy. We hold within our hearts the highest regard for the founders, pastors, staff, and congregation. May this record serve to preserve the memory of a wonderful ministry. May it serve as a prophetic reminder of the faithfulness of God and the stewardship of a people. May it also serve as notice of the consequences of deviating from the course set by the Lord.

We intend to answer three strategic questions that continue to surround the legacy of this work and our involvement until the very end: *Did the ministry finish its course? Did the ministry come to a tragic end? Why did we remain until the end?*

We are releasing this record now because of a Divine mandate. This is our perspective and our journey. Travel with us as we navigate through time and revisit the moments, events, people, and place that came to be known as the Cathedral of the Holy Spirit.

Table of Contents

Prologue

On a sweltering Sunday morning on August 16, 2009, I had preached one of the last two messages that would be delivered in the massive neo-Gothic structure called the Cathedral of the Holy Spirit. The property had been sold to a very progressive Baptist Church after the death of the primary leader and founder, Earl Paulk, Jr. By now, the clouds of allegations and suspicions of sexual misconduct had almost eclipsed nearly 60 years of productive and successful ministry. Now, a congregation that once had over 12,000 members from different races, cultures, and ethnic groups had dwindled to less than 300 predominantly Black members. A ministry that had once touched nations through its message and ministry programs had finally come to an end. We had been a part of the work for 30 years. My role as a resident pastor and a bishop had allowed me to experience the rise of the ministry from obscurity to becoming a household name. We were there when Pastor Paulk had the dream of the Kingdom that radically changed the course and identity of the entire ministry. We were there when a predominantly White congregation was transformed into a multi-racial group of committed people. We were there during the exciting years of a youth ministry called Alpha that invaded homes, schools and communities with its brand of evangelism. We were there when drama, choreographed dancing, mime, art and innovative brands of music such as rock, jazz, classical and rap were introduced into the public worship agenda. We were there when Bishop Robert McAlister of Brazil ordained Pastor Paulk a bishop without vestments or any elaborate liturgy before a growing and excited congregation. We were there when notable prophets and apostles came with words and deeds that stirred our creativity and predicted the global influence of the ministry and the construction of a most unusual place of worship. We were there during the days of the great circus tent that housed the ministry during one of the hottest summers and the coldest winter while a new construction was underway. We were there when a congregation literally became a construction crew to build a transitional worship space called the K-Center that became too small too soon to house a rapidly growing church. We were there during the death and burial of some of our beloved elders, friends, and members. We were there during the first world conference on the *Kingdom of God* that attracted over 80 nations and some of the most noted speakers of that day. We were there the first day the Cathedral opened with a capacity crowd of over 12,000 people to hear the first message preached by Archbishop Paulk titled *Whosoever Will, Let Him Come*. We were there during the international conferences when leaders from Africa, Asia, Australia, Europe, South America, Caribbean and the United States came annually for ten days of teaching and training. We were there when the scandals became public and every news agency converged upon the property as thousands of people and several leaders left and the entire ministry was jeopardized. We were there during the years of hopelessness, despair, disillusionment, and confusion when prophetic words promising recovery and restoration were received with skepticism and disbelief. We were there when the young heir apparent left with some young leaders and members of congregation to start another church. We were there when the young leader returned. We were there when the leadership of the church was transferred from Archbishop Paulk to a son of the ministry. We were there during the many prayer vigils that were held for the ministry. We were there the Sunday morning during the announcement of the death of Archbishop Paulk. On this particular Sunday morning in August before the final relocation to another site, I stood before a remnant congregation of 300 and delivered a message titled *Navigating the Journey*. With deliberate intent, punctuated, at times, with tears and brief moments of humor, I chronicled the history and legacy of this ministry and made some predictions about its future. My work was done, and my association with the ministry was complete. I had gathered a few pictures and memoires that would serve as a reminder of epic moments and over 30 years of ministry life. The few leaders and people that remained were moving in another direction, and we would not be accompanying them. We did not leave them; rather, they left us. As I looked out over the small congregation nestled strategically down front in those padded pews that had once accommodated thousands of people, my mind recaptured memories of meetings, conferences, and people who were now a part of history. There were no regrets, but joy and peace were desperately competing with any sadness or disappointment that sought to enter my thoughts.

We stayed until the very end because the Lord directed us. Despite all the allegations, questions, and suspicions regarding our continued stewardship roles in the ministry, we never considered leaving. A major prophet counseled us to leave at the advent of the last scandal; otherwise, he warned that we would be slandered and lose credibility among the churches. While we thought the counsel was correct, there had been two admonitions given to us at the beginning of this journey in 1980. One was simply to never defend ourselves despite any accusation or misrepresentation of our character, motivation, or intention. There were many opportunities to violate this command during the journey and especially during the latter days when we reached out to those who exposed the scandal. We were accused of being friends with the alleged enemies of the ministry. The other command was akin to the admonition of Paul to Timothy. The apostles cautioned the young leader to endure hardness and not be entangled with the affairs of this life (2 Tim. 2:3-4). We never considered the implications of such warnings during our journey. Nevertheless, there is no precedent in Scripture where the Lord removed a prophet from among His people when they were in trouble.

Admittedly, we were indeed disappointed, saddened, and even angered by the final disposition of the work, but at the end of the journey, we were powerless to change the course. Even though the new leadership designated us as being a part of the "old school," there was no internal friction nor tension between any of us as leaders. I had given prophetic words of hope and possibility from this same podium, and some were not being fulfilled according to my expectations. I was at peace with those unfilled predictions, for I knew that they were conditional and demanded repentance. I would later realize that the burden of prophetic fulfillment does not rest upon the shoulders of the messenger but upon the recipients. Thus, my final words on that Sunday morning were a celebration of our history as a people and a prayer for the future for those who were moving in different directions. I expressed my thanksgiving to God for His faithfulness, grace and mercy, and for the privilege He had given us to participate in this wonderful legacy. Surely, an old phase had ended and a new one had begun.

It has now been five years since that Sunday morning in August 2009. The memories have not faded nor have they been wasted.

CHAPTER 1

THE BEGINNING PLACE

I was born in an old farmhouse in a tiny southern rural town called Newnan by a midwife. It was a natural birth, and I was told I would have died later of whooping cough had it not been for one of my aunts who literally ran three miles to the nearest telephone to contact a doctor. She constantly reminds me of that story. My grandmother, who was a godly woman, was a witness to my birth, and she prayed over me and asked the Lord to let me be a preacher and a doctor. Later in life, she gave me a small Bible containing the words of that prayer.

As the years progressed, I attended Turner High School in Atlanta, Georgia. All the students and teachers were Black since the public school system and the colleges were segregated during those days. Hamilton Holmes and Charlene Hunter, who had recently graduated from Turner High School in 1959, integrated the University of Georgia in 1961. Upon graduation in 1961, I was selected with four of my classmates to integrate Georgia Institute of Technology in Atlanta. The process of integration required federal troops to intervene because of the violence created by the White students and teachers. Because of the danger surrounding the integration of those schools, my parents directed me to Morehouse College. It was a much better place for me.

During my freshman year at Morehouse, I met a beautiful young high school senior named Sandra Childs. The next year, she became a student at Spelman College, which is located directly across the street from Morehouse College. We married while in college and moved in with Sandra's mother until we both graduated. I worked part-time at a trucking company to provide income. After our graduation, Sandra became employed as a public school teacher. I continued working at the trucking company and later acquired a job in communication at Western Electric. Those were happy days, for our future was all before us, but a career loading freight on trucks and writing specifications for engineers were not exciting career aspirations. Neither one of those positions provided me with the psychological and spiritual stimulation I needed for growth. In my effort to launch another career that would better utilize my skills and stimulate my interest, I interviewed with a pharmaceutical company that required relocation either to New York or Detroit. The winter weather in both places was too cold and never seemed to end. So, out of pure frustration, I decided to make inquiries about a possible career in dentistry. Providence fell, and through a series of events, I was accepted for the freshman class at Howard University School of Dentistry.

In 1970 when President Nixon was in office, I never dreamed that we would live in the shadows of the White House and the Smithsonian Institute. Yet, during the sweltering month of August, Sandra and I packed up our two children and all our earthly possessions and moved to Washington, DC, to spend the next four years in new environment. At that time, we did not realize that the persistent pain that Sandra had been experiencing for months before we left Atlanta was a tumor. Furthermore, we were totally unaware that our one-year-old daughter had a genetic heart disorder. Fortunately, my role as a sophomore dental student and Sandra's position at a large hospital made health care available and more affordable. The Chief of Cardiology at Howard University School of Medicine and two very prominent surgeons also provided surgical care for Gina and Sandra at no cost. In retrospect, I am thoroughly convinced that this was providential and that the source of their health care resided in Washington and not in Atlanta.

After I graduated with honors, we relocated to Boston for a two-year post-doctorate program in prosthetic dentistry. Boston was turbulent and violent because public schools were being integrated. There were daily reports of racial conflicts and gang violence. Traffic jams were prevalent in the early morning rush hours because protesters entered the main expressways and drove their cars slow. And in additions to the social climate, the cold winters were challenging. We lived in a little town called Duxbury where we thoroughly enjoyed two years of snow and all the history of Plymouth, Salem, Martha's Vineyard and Provident Town. We attended a church located an hour's drive from our home. It was a good two years, and all the people and experiences enlarged the dimensions of our world. Right before we left Duxbury for a teaching assignment at Howard University School of Dentistry, Sandra and I were awakened one night, and we saw a Bible encircled by a bright light at the foot of our bed. It was certainly an unusual experience and the meaning of that vision would come later.

Shortly thereafter, we were back in the Washington, DC area for what we thought would be two years. It was an exciting time, and we leased a home in Maryland. Then we discovered that the pastor of the church where we had attended in Massachusetts had been relocated to a church in Baltimore, Maryland. Needless to say, Sandra and I became very involved in that church. During that year, we were introduced to another interesting phenomenon that would radically change our lives. While attending a Women's Aglow meeting in Baltimore, Maryland, Sandra and I received a prophecy about our future in ministry. At that stage in our lives, we knew nothing about ministry except that it involved a church and a pastorate. But Sandra and I had been searching to understand the desire within us to study the Bible and to know more about the things of God. The prophecy made public the desires of our hearts and even promised that the Lord would give us wisdom and knowledge. That was surprising and perplexing to us, for we had never had someone say that we would be in the ministry. That same evening our pastor also gave us a prophecy that we were called into the ministry and that it was not a traditional pulpit ministry but, nevertheless, it was a call. Back then, the call into the ministry was to a church, a pastorate and to contend with deacons, the congregation and board members. All of this was new to us and there was very little understanding of the meaning behind those events. I had forgotten the prayer of my grandmother during my birth when she asked the Lord to make me a preacher and a doctor. However, the vision of the Bible encircled by light was beginning to take on meaning. We sought to start a dental practice and purchase a home that first year in Maryland, but providence was at work, and all plans were hindered. Although we were saddened at first, it all began to make sense, for such a commitment would have prevented our next step. At the end of a year, we were packing again and heading back to Atlanta.

We had been away for seven years, but all our family and friends were still in Atlanta. We leased a home in Southwest Atlanta, and settled down for a career of living, and joined the United Methodist Church near our home. Soon we were actively involved in the choir. The pastor would regularly call upon me to pray for the congregation on Sundays, and he would also invite me to stand alongside of him as he prayed over the seemingly endless stream of people that presented themselves for prayer. In fact, I became the outreach ministry of the church and drove the van to pick up an elderly man every Sunday morning. I met him while visiting a family member in the hospital. He was resting on a bed in the hall while waiting for a room. As I passed by him, I felt compelled to stop and pray with him. His name was Mr. Watson, and he had recently had both his legs amputated and could no longer be the truck driver that he had been for so many years. That brief moment led to a year of picking him up every Sunday morning and taking him home at the end of the meetings. He seemed to enjoy the church, and the people loved him. On one of my regular trips to pick him up early on Sunday, as usual, his wife met me at the door and announced that he had passed away early that morning. I remember how she cried and thanked me for making the last year of his life so happy. I was thankful for that year, too.

The religious communities of Atlanta were alive but still polarized along the lines of race and culture. However, there were signs of the "browning of the churches." That is, churches that had traditionally been all Black or all White were integrating.

The Charismatic Renewal and the outpouring of the Holy Spirit among Catholic and Protestant Churches were quite noticeable in some of those churches that we visited. The Full Gospel Business Men Association hosted weekly and monthly meetings at restaurants and large halls that attracted hundreds and thousands of people. The Word of Faith Movement was very active, and Atlanta hosted some of the most prominent speakers such as Kenneth Hagin, Fred Price, Kenneth Copeland, Marilyn Hickey, Charles Capps and others. Sandra and I visited many of those meetings in a quest to understand the world of faith and spiritual ministration of prophecies and miracles. Interestingly, enough, we received prophetic words about ministry while attending several of those meetings. In fact, I received the Baptism of the Holy Spirit in 1978 at a house meeting. While Sandra had always been the spiritual one, there was a growing urge in both of us to study the Scriptures, even more. Christian bookstores became our hang out where we purchased everything written by Kenneth Hagin, Fred Price, Marilyn Hickey and other Word of Faith ministers. We even entertained the idea of attending Bible School. In fact, one of the presidents of a local seminary attended our church and encouraged us to enroll. For some reason, we felt restrained. Shortly thereafter, we began a Bible study at our home with a couple, our two children and a dog named King. The dog left but the couple stayed, and the people began to come every Friday night. The crowd exceeded the capacity of our basement, so we relocated the meetings to a larger building.

While employment as a staff dentist at a local health center provided income, we made plans to start our full-time private practice. We had decided on a beautiful location in downtown Atlanta, selected the equipment, and receive preliminary approval of the business loan. Everything was in motion, and suddenly, the process stopped. The loan that was previously approved was mysteriously disapproved. Indeed, the loan officer was perplexed over the rejection. Sandra and I were also perplexed and greatly disappointed over this turn of events. Most of the young dentists that I knew were actively engaged in their practices. Whenever I attended a meeting of the local dental society, all of the beautiful expensive cars were a testimonial of some very successful dental practices. I always parked my old red and white Chevrolet away from the display of Rolls Royce, Mercedes, Bentleys and Cadillacs. Whenever I attended any of the meetings, I had to always entertain the various inquiries about my new practice, which was always in the plans and never seemed to have an address.

Nevertheless, things were about to change and understanding was about to reveal itself. It started one morning in my office at the health center. As I was glancing out the window and entertaining thoughts about the future, I was impressed with the simple thought to trust the Lord. At that time, there were no other options. It was during those days that Oral Roberts was soliciting funds for the construction of the City of Faith in Tulsa, Oklahoma. We were excited about the work at Oral Roberts University, so we attended one of the seminars on the beautiful campus. It was during that visit that we came in contact with two ORU Seminary students who invited us to visit their home church in Decatur, Georgia, which was about twenty miles from our home. It was Chapel Hill Harvester Church, a classical Pentecostal church with a predominantly all-white congregation.

After our first visit, we made arrangement to meet with the senior pastor, Earl Paulk. He was a very confident leader with roots in Church of God in Cleveland, Tennessee. He also had a history of involvement in the civil rights movements in Atlanta. The meeting ended with an invitation for me to preach at the church. It would be a regular Wednesday night meeting and the crowd would be smaller than the Sunday service. When we arrived, however, the parking lot was burdened with cars, and people occupied every available seat and space along the walls of the sanctuary. I don't remember on what topic I preached, but once I finished, Pastor Paulk literally rushed to the podium and announced that Sandra and I we were a part of his ministry.

Sandra and I had been actively looking for a church home, and I had a dream of a church building with a gravel driveway in front. In my dream, the altar area of the church was encircled with a beautiful black railed fence about four feet tall. After these whirlwind encounters that began with a simple appointment and a preaching assignment, I had anticipated that Pastor Paulk would call me again. Furthermore, I had also made up my mind that I would accept whatever he asked of me. Indeed, within a few days, he called and invited me to breakfast. It was during that morning meeting that the vision in Boston, the prophecies in Maryland, and the decline of my dental loan in Atlanta began to take on meaning. He offered me a position as a pastor at the church and promised that the salary would be no where near what I earned as a dentist. I accepted the invitation the first time because I had been impressed to do whatever he asked of me. I remembered that he looked a little startled and did not believe that I understood the salary limitation, so he repeated himself several times. It was then that I revealed to him the events I had encountered in Boston, Maryland, and Atlanta. If I had started a private practice in Maryland or Atlanta, I could not have started this journey. I immediately resigned my full-time position at the health center and maintained my part-time practice, which was located about two miles from the church. Incidentally, once I came on staff and shared my dream of the church, one of the senior pastors excitedly announced the similarity with the old church before the parking lot was finished. With new understanding of the past, the next dimension of our journey would begin.

CHAPTER 2

A TWIG AND A TREE

Our early years at the church were times of growth and exposure to things of God and the daily operation of a local church. It was a predominantly all-white ministry in the South that was about to undergo a radical transformation in its principles, practices, and associations. I was privileged to work closely with Pastor Paulk in my role as one of the pastors and as the leader of our newly formed network of churches. He was a dominant and very effective pastor. He understood the people and strategies needed to grow an effective and relevant ministry. It became obvious to me very early that a lot of things could be accomplished in this ministry if no one cared who received the credit. My personality did not command me to be the leader, and to me, cooperation works better than competition. This was not the same for all of our pastors for some of them had been senior leaders of ministries before they joined our staff. They had been accustomed to giving directions and establishing priorities. The experience of serving under a dominant leader who needed to lead without the distractions of competition was a challenge for some. Nevertheless, if the ministry were to thrive, there could be no internal competition nor would there be any toleration by the senior Paulk of other visions contrary to the central one.

During the early years, we had regular meetings with

the leaders and staff. I quickly learned that consistent communication with associates and staff was critical for the continuity of purpose. Those were years of the planning, writing vision statements, and identifying the gifts and callings that were among us. It was exciting to work in an environment with such committed people who had energy and zeal, and I was an eager student who observed and recorded what I saw and heard. In fact, I wrote my first book, titled *The Second* during those early years, and it was my personal observations of the evolution of this ministry and the consolidation of different people, ideas, and thoughts into a common purpose. The most critical factor in the process would be trust. I remember a conversation with Pastor Paulk after one our long presbytery meetings, which usually lasted for three to four hours. As we left the meeting, he turned to me and said, "Kirby, the Lord has shown me in the Spirit that you are a man of God whom I can trust." I was thankful for the complement, but I was not so sure of its ultimate meaning. Other intimate moments like that one revealed more of his heart.

As the work grew, my knowledge of pastoral ministry expanded. I was excited about visiting the sick, counseling members, and meeting with deacons and caregivers in our home. We were learning more about the origin and foundation of this church called Chapel Hill Harvester. Pastor Paulk would often make reference to two Scriptural references that established the name and the mission of the ministry:

> *"But when he saw the multitudes, he was moved with compassion on them, because they fainted, and*

were scattered abroad as sheep having no shepherd.
Then saith he unto his disciples, the harvest truly is
plenteous, but the labourers are few; pray ye therefore
the Lord of the harvest, that he will send forth
labourers into his harvest. " Matthew 9:36-38

From this Scripture came the name "harvester" which was the basis of the ministry: Chapel Hill Harvester Church. The strength of the ministry would be the obedience of its leaders to God and their compassion for people. The willingness of its leaders to respond to the commands of the Lord regardless of the time, season, or circumstances proved to be the greatest asset and strength. We accepted all who were estranged from their denominations or anyone who was marginalized, alienated, confused, or ignorant of the power of God's redemption. The laborers would be five-fold ministers, a trans-cultural congregation, and a host of innovative and creative ministries. This would include music, song, dance, drama, radio, television, and the various outreach ministries to government, churches, and nations. It would include the formation of various networks such as The International Communion of Churches and The Harvester Network of Churches. A pivotal mandate in the minds of the founders was to restore individuals and ministries that had stumbled and fallen. We had no idea of the future implications of these thoughts.

The other significant Scriptural reference is found in the prophetic literature:

"Thus saith the Lord God: I will also take of the highest branch of the high cedar, and will set it; I will crop off from the top of his young twigs a tender one, and will plant it upon a high mountain and eminent; in the mountain of the height of Israel will I plant it, and it shall bring forth boughs, and bear fruit, and be a goodly cedar, and under it shall dwell all fowl of every wing, and in the shadows of the branches thereof shall they dwell. And all the trees of the field shall know that I the Lord have brought down the high tree, have exalted the low tree, have dried upon the green tree and have made the dry tree to flourish. I the Lord have spoken and have done it." Ezekiel 17:22-24

Historically, this prophetic Word has reference to the nation of Israel, but in a contemporary sense, it could be compared to Chapel Hill Harvester Church. For Pastor Earl Paulk, an adherent of the Church of God, Cleveland, Tennessee (the great tree), came to Decatur, Georgia, in the late 1960s to a rural area that was dense with trees. There he was directed of the Lord to take the branch of one of the trees (Church of God) and plant it (a branch with roots in Pentecost) in the ground as a sign of the work that was about to begin (the first building constructed stands approximately in that location). For the Lord would begin a ministry that would influence both the sacred and secular world with its ideas and practices. The symbolism of fowls of every wing dwelling in the shadow of the tree is, indeed, indicative of the influence of the ministry upon every type of nation, church, and ministry. Indeed, all the other trees, the churches and ministries would come to know that the Lord had exalted this ministry as a tool to proclaim and demonstrate the presence, power, and influence of the Kingdom of God at a local church level. For the field is the world, the power is the Holy Spirit, the wisdom and knowledge of God is the Scripture and the agency is the church.

Interestingly, it was during one of our long presbytery meetings, that I gave a prophecy using this same Scriptural reference. I remember that the room was filled with intense joy and excitement as Pastor Paulk sounded out a response to the prophecy and encouraged all in attendance to hear it.

I remember meeting with Pastor Paulk in his office and sharing a prophetic insight concerning the future of the ministry. At the time, he was content to be a local pastor in Decatur, Georgia. He had no concern for travelling or developing ministry beyond the local church. For me, the field was the world, and being behind a desk in an office for eight hours was not my idea of ministry. There had to be a way to integrate these two perspectives. So, that morning in his office, I shared the thoughts that the ministry of this local church was about to expand and that he would become known around the world. His response was not too enthusiastic, but I persisted. I reminded him of the original vision and the experience that he had so often shared with us about the twig and the tree. From this small branch would come a ministry that would touch the world. My words to him were cordially accepted, but he still did not have that desire. However, a vision in the night was about to change all of that.

CHAPTER 3

WEEPING IN THE NIGHT AND THE KINGDOM IN THE MORNING

We were about to discover that God does not take a lot of time to make changes. We were a typical Charismatic Church with Pentecostal roots, but we were not rolling on the floor or doing marathon sprints through the aisles. In fact, order was a dominant theme in those days. There was very little room for individual creativity and innovation in worship among the congregation. The choir wore its beautiful robes and even sang from hymnals with some occasional creative music. There was no choreographed dancing, and our youth ministry, Alpha, provided most of the excitement. This group of young high school and college-age kids was the evangelistic outreach of the church. The members infiltrated the school systems and the communities with their enthusiasm, music, and creativity. The preaching and teaching of Pastor Paulk was extraordinary. In addition, there were the regular ministry of Iverna Thompkins and Judson Cornwall and they were internationally acclaimed ministers. As a church, we were comfortable, and ordinary, but everything was about to change.

A Vision in the Night

After a usual week, we all gathered for our normal Sunday morning services, but we were met by a weeping prophet. Pastor Paulk had experienced a vision in the night that was to radically change his life and the ministry of the entire church. I would be privileged to experience firsthand a reformation in a local church that would affect the world. A predominantly all-white congregation was about to be transformed into a multi-racial, trans-cultural ministry. An emphasis was about to be placed on a five-fold ministry, Holy Spirit dynamic, expressive worship, liturgy, and socially active ministry programs. In time, the local congregation of Chapel Hill Harvester Church would become known simply as the "Cathedral of the Holy Spirit." A neo-gothic cathedral would ultimately be constructed to house a congregation that would exceed 12,000 members who would worship God in psalms, hymns, spiritual songs, and make melodies in their hearts. This ministry was about to demonstrate the implication of Kingdom theology upon church architecture and ministry.[1]

A dream in the night precipitated a significant change in some of the theological views and practices.[2] Long standing beliefs of the Kingdom of God as a future hope and the church as a colony of redeemed people awaiting their deliverance from this present world was about to be radically transformed.[3] The significance of the First Coming of Jesus and the implications upon the life and ministry of the church was about to take on a different meaning. First of all, while classical Pentecostalism had emphasized the Second Coming of the Lord as the supreme event to which all else was preparatory, the finished work of Jesus was given priority. Second, the gospel that was preached by Jesus and the apostles would assume a primary place in the preaching agenda of the church. Fresh revelatory meaning would be given to such phrases as "thy kingdom come, they will be done on earth as it is in heaven" (Matt. 6:10); and "held in the heaven until the restitution of all things" (Acts 3:19-21). Attention would be given to words such as "witness," "occupy," "disciple," "salt," and "light." The boundary line between the sacred sphere of the Church and the secular sphere of the world would be erased, and the concept of a prophetic community would be presented.[4] The church would no longer to be a "cultural critic" that denounced the problems of war, crime, immorality, and disorganization in the world as simply expressions of Divine judgment against human rebellion.[5] Instead, the church would become a "cultural architect," empowered by the Holy Spirit, to offer solutions through the proclamations and demonstrations of the principles of the Kingdom of God in the midst of a confused world. A theology of escape would be exchanged for a theology of influence, and instead of avoiding those "secular occupations" such as law, politics, education, science, athletics, entertainment, and commerce, the members of the church would be strongly encouraged to assume their stewardship responsibilities in all of these areas.[6]

A vision in the night would cause us to blend theological concepts with practical strategies through a newly established educational system. Education would be viewed as an evangelistic strategy. Consequently, a school of theology would be established and open to all. Its intent would not be simply to produce preachers but to also equip the "laity" with the tools to transform their world through practical and applied theological instructions. An elementary and a high school would be initiated to provide an opportunity to merge secular education with sound Biblical ideas, and the majority of the school's graduates would enter college.

This vision in the night would provoke us to rethink our mission. We thought that salvation of the individual was the center of God's will, but we would discover that it is not the circumference. We would hear the prophet Habakkuk declaring that the earth is to be filled with knowledge of the glory of the Lord. This mandate would include not only individuals but also institutions, organizations, laws, legislation, and government. This newly discovered theology of the Kingdom of God would focus the attention of evangelism to include soul winning, church planting and cultural transforming. Consequently, we would develop programs to facilitate the rehabilitation of the individual and task forces of elders and members of the congregation that would actively engage the political community in dialogue to fashion solution-oriented programs for the various challenges facing the community. A political task force would eventually be organized to research and examine legislation and activities in the political sector that affected the Cathedral and the community. Politicians and other social leaders would be invited to discuss their programs with the leadership and before the congregation. The Cathedral, as the local church, would, indeed, become the evangelistic center of a region and also the center of social and environmental change. In fact, with a congregation that would eventually include people from almost every profession, the message of the Cathedral would greatly influenced the members who were builders and construction engineers. Residential communities would be designed and developed to eliminate the polarization of people according to age, race, culture, and socioeconomic status. This vision in the night would change everything.

What we did not know at the time was that when you pray for the Kingdom of God to come and His will be done on earth as it is in heaven, you are asking for trouble! It is a prayer for a cosmic conflict in which light confronts darkness, truth collides with heresies, crooked places are made straight and rough places are made plain. The answer to this prayer could be seen over and over again. In fact, the morning that Pastor Paulk shared some of these views, a large number of members left the church. I was not greatly disturbed by this turn of events. Even though I was not accustomed to church splits or defections, I did not spend a lot of time thinking about the events of that morning. Nevertheless, I can say that *weeping in the night does not always bring joy in the morning.*

Vision Meets Old Attitudes and New Opportunities

Unfortunately, there were some things that the *vision in the night* did not change. For example, Pastor Paulk believed in male authority and female submission. Although were reformer and had championed the liberation of the down-trodden, the poor, and anyone who had been estranged because of his or her personal failures and mistakes, they still believed that men should rule. They did not care much for strong women who used their emotions to control men. They would often encourage men, both single and married, to help single women who had children with repairs on their automobiles, and maintenance of their houses. If the wives complained, they were accused of being jealous and selfish. Such comments from the pulpit posed threats to the female members. While Pastor Paulk allowed some women to function in ministry, he firmly believed in a patriarchal structure.

Because my roots were not in Pentecost, this model of social relationship was new to me. In fact, this philosophy of male dominance put me in conflict with Sandra. We had lived in an egalitarian relationship all our married life, but they had been in ministry for years, and I was searching to understand things that I did not know. These were times of confusion and emotional stress for us because we were living between two contrasting environments, patriarchy in the church and equality in my home. Furthermore, a small percentage of the pastors and the congregation embraced the same ideas of female submission, male headship and authority in the church and the home. Sandra, however, stood her ground, and not one moment did she entertain such ideas. She had done extensive research on creational order and gender equality, and I was reading all the material as well. In fact, we were in the process of gathering material for a new book titled *And He Gave Them*.

We had discovered that misinterpretations of the creation narrative in Genesis and misuse of words such as head, helpmeet, submission, covering and authority had put women at risk in the church, market place and home. This gender equality that Sandra and I had shared throughout our marriage was under attack. Why would God give women such abilities and powers of creativity and demand that they submit to men and not be allowed to make independent decisions outside of the "covering" of some man? Those constant references to male dominance and the threat that men who did not have their wives in submission would lose their anointing put my marriage under stress. Sandra and I stood our ground and modeled our egalitarian relationship in every aspect of the ministry. When I counseled members of the congregation in my office at church, I would often include Sandra in the meeting. We created husband/wife deacon teams. We simply lived publicly as we lived privately. In retrospect, I firmly believe that this faulty concept of male dominance and female submission contributed to the sexual immorality.

In spite of the issue of patriarchy being unchanged in the minds and hearts of many in our church leadership, this *dream in the night* and *Kingdom in the morning* would bring tremendous global attention to Pastor Earl Paulk and the local church, now called the Cathedral of the Holy Spirit. There would be television appearances on Jim Bakker broadcasts and visits by high profile ministers, such as Oral Roberts, Ern Baxter, Benson Idahosa, Kelly Varner, Tom Skiner and others who would precipitate the beginning of a world class ministry. The ministry would be a source of compassion, comfort and wisdom during some of the most difficult times in the Atlanta/ Decatur area. This was especially evident when a number of Black boys were abducted and murdered. Pastor Paulk and the congregation were involved in the resolution of that terrible crisis. When two White women were assaulted by two Black men and one of the women died, there was racial tension in the city. Pastor Paulk and I visited the bedside of one of the victims and spoke to the news media. This, I am certain, averted a potentially volatile racial conflict.

The concept of the Kingdom of God, indeed, affected the attitude and behavior of our local church toward hurting people. We developed ministries of compassion for those who were addicted to drugs and alcohol, those who had destructive behavior, and those whose lifestyles put them in conflict with cultural norms. For example, the AIDS epidemic became a national and international challenge and lack of understanding of the cause and transmission caused the public to panic. While, today, we understand much about the disease, there was a time when the public felt that the disease could be easily transmitted by a kiss, being in proximity to a victim or touching a piece of clothing or artifact. We discovered that AIDS victims and HIV positive individuals were a part of our congregation. Thus, the lack of information and presence of false information precipitated a great concern among our congregation. We were a church that greeted one another with a hug and a kiss on the cheek. Were we in danger of the disease being transmitted among the members? This controversy demanded a response from the church, so Bishop Paulk preached a message on compassion that conditioned the minds and attitudes of the congregation toward the crisis. As for me, I was treating dental patients who were HIV positive. Thus, this concern was extensive for many of us.

The crisis did not only affect our congregation, but it also raged among other churches. There were theological and doctrinal controversies. Was AIDS a Divine judgment against homosexuality? Was it an end time sign? The answers to these questions generated factions. I was asked to address the issue of AIDS at a church leadership conference. During my presentation, a few members of a Gay Rights Group entered the meeting and began to denounce the church and claim that Christians were insensitive and unresponsive to the AIDS crisis. I was disturbed and angered by their intrusion and accusations. I felt they were trying to force their position upon the entire group and were making accusations without the facts. Since I was speaking when they entered the meeting, the two hundred pastors and leaders looked to me to respond. First of all, I welcomed them to the meeting even though it was a registered conference. Secondly, I challenged their stereotyping of the entire church simply because a few churches had been unresponsive to the AID crisis because of ignorance and fear. Thirdly, I informed them that we were presently addressing the very issue of AIDS at the moment they stormed into the meeting. And finally, I rehearsed my belief that AIDS was not a judgment against homosexuality since it was affecting individuals outside of the gay community and even unborn infants. When one of the activists openly admitted that he had AIDS, I asked if I could pray for him. He consented, and I went over to where he was standing and embraced him and prayed. He wept, and I could sense his fear, pain, and rejection.

That encounter taught me a great deal. While I was initially disturbed by the intrusion, I discovered that the correction of ignorance was information. For that reason, I wrote one of the first papers in our ministry on AIDS and the responsibility of the local church. AIDS was not peculiar to the gay community, and it was not a Divine judgment from God. I also set forth the idea of the church as a healing community where all people were welcomed. Since we were people of faith and believed in healing, there needed to be some understanding of how faith and medicine work together. Faith is not irrational, nor is it a denial of reality. As a result, several of our local pastors organized ministry teams of volunteers to visit the hospitals and hospice facilities and minister to the AIDS patients and their families and friends. While being mindful of hospital protocol, we initiated a protocol of compassion.

These experiences taught me invaluable lessons. Fear is often a product of ignorance, and prejudice is often a lack of exposure to other people and environments. Compassion and sensitivity must be cultivated. My dental education had allowed Sandra and me to experience people from different racial, cultural and ethnic groups. As a health care provider, I was trained to treat all people regardless of their status in life. For us, the dimensions of our world had increased because of the people and ideas that we had included. However, this was not true for those who lacked the knowledge and experience of other cultures and environment.

New Leader, New Attitude

I was often asked whether the success and exposure of the ministry of the Cathedral influenced Bishop Paulk. While the *vision in the night* changed his ministry perspectives and brought tremendous public visibility and global recognition, it did not seem to change the very nature of the man. In my judgment, Bishop Earl Paulk disciplined himself in humility before God, and he enlarged the borders of his world to include other people. I observed this when Bishop John Meares, the uncle of Clariece Paulk, introduced him to Bishop Robert McAllister of Brazil. Bishop McAllister had been ordained to his office of bishop by a special synod of the Roman Catholic Church. Historically, Pentecostals have not been friendly with Roman Catholics.

When Bishop McAllister visited our church and saw

the influence of this ministry, he was very impressed and recommended the consecration of Pastor Paulk to the office of bishop. Pastor Paulk always insisted that he was called and ordained as a pastor and that pastoring was his primary ministry. Yet, on a Sunday morning before the local congregation, he was ordained to the office of bishop without vestments or liturgy. It was like a chapter in the book of Acts when Paul and Barnabas were set forth with prayer and the laying on of hands of those present. The consecration of Earl Paulk took place in a few minutes before our local congregation with prayer and the ministration of the Holy Spirit. I still remember the words of Bishop McAllister to the newly consecrated Bishop Paulk: "Sir, I do you no favor!"

Pastor Paulk became Bishop Paulk, yet he remained approachable. While I had very little understanding of the office of bishop and the liturgy, the events of that morning impressed me and greatly influenced my philosophy of ministry. The preeminence of the Holy Spirit and the simplicity of the moment would have a lasting effect upon me. This was evident years later after I was ordained a bishop under similar simplistic circumstances and later became responsible for the consecration of bishops and elders. In fact, my ordination took place on a Sunday morning without any previous announcement. During a casual conversation in Bishop Paulk's office on a Friday, he made me aware of his plans to ordain me to the office of bishop. My response was simply, "If it took more than five minutes, then it was not God." There were no vestments nor elaborate liturgy. With Sandra at my side, Bishop Paulk, the founding leaders and the presbytery laid hands on me and prayed before our congregation. I remember the comments made by Sandra during the ceremony. She said, "This is the Lord's doing, and it is marvelous in our sight."

The events of that morning would greatly influence my concept of ordination. In fact, I was a part of the consecration of the first Pentecostal bishop in Estonia. The organizers had planned a very extensive liturgical service with all of the vestments. In addition to a very large congregation, there were bishops from the Greek Orthodox, Roman Catholic, Assemblies of God, and Russian Orthodox faiths. As each bishop discharged his designated role in the service with deliberate and calculated grace, the congregation was silent. It was not until I began to minister in prophecy that a presence seemed to sweep through that great cathedral, and suddenly, all of the bishops and the people began to lift their hands and worship the Lord with tears and shouts of adoration. Even now, I recall those moments with reverence and thanksgiving to God for that day in 1981 when Earl Paulk was set forth as a bishop with simplicity and the ministration of the Holy Spirit.

Often, I have been asked if the extensive public exposure and popularity given to the ministry of Earl Paulk were contributing factors to his misbehavior. In my judgment, I firmly believe that he handled the notoriety traps quite well, and he did not allow the national and international attention to influence him. However, there must have been convictions and beliefs within the man that finally manifested themselves. He still remained a pioneer for justice and liberation of all who were oppressed. He also willingly offered any assistance possible to pastors and leaders who were within and without the Pentecostal/Charismatic dimension. For example, he was among the first to visit Jim Bakker during his imprisonment.

I remember how Archbishop Benson Idahosa of Nigeria sent one of his leaders to the church to be trained. The young man was not only trained, but he was also well cared for during the entire year. In fact, the Archbishop would later leave two of his children in the care of the Paulk family while they received their education at our school. While success can change some individuals, Earl Paulk seemed to have understood greatness, which was to be a servant to all. This impressed me and instilled in me that the strong should always reach out to the weak, and to whom much is given, much is required. God is the source of all, and without Him, we can do nothing that is lasting or beneficial. It is perhaps for these and other reasons why I addressed Earl Paulk as "the Good Bishop."

Indeed, a *vision in the night* and *Kingdom in the morning* had a tremendous effect.

CHAPTER 4

THE BODY OF CHRIST IS ONE

When Sandra and I arrived at the Cathedral, a predominantly an all-white congregation, prejudice was still the norm in the South. Our church sat at the back door of the prestigious Stone Mountain, which was once the gathering place for the Klu Klux Clan. Interestingly, enough, during my second year at the church, I was selected to serve on the all-white Stone Mountain Memorial Board. This gave me an opportunity to sit alongside of several of the former governors and legislators of Georgia. During one of the social gatherings of the Board, Sandra and I had the privilege of meeting Governor Lester Maddox, a former governor who had created quite a disturbance during his tenure in office. Indeed, he was known for wielding an ax handle and being a staunch segregationist. He was very frail and was only a shadow of the figure that had filled the front pages of the *Atlanta Journal and Constitution* newspaper for years. Now he was standing before us and confessing that he was not a segregationist and did not hate Black people. He said all of that display was simply a political strategy to gain votes and maintain his popularity with power brokers. As I reflected on those brief moments, I could

31

still hear that distinct southern dialect as he repented for his past behavior. He passed away a few months later.

In addition to the reconciliation of social conflicts, the leadership of the Cathedral took deliberate steps to reconcile the various factions in the Body of Christ.[7] This effort to integrate the contribution of three streams of Christian traditions came to be known as a "convergence movement."[8] These three streams included the Roman Catholic tradition with an emphasis on orthodoxy and the importance of liturgy and sacraments; the Reformed tradition, which stressed the centrality of the Scripture, personal faith, and the importance of the proclaimed Word of God, and the Pentecostal tradition, which emphasized the baptism of the Holy Spirit as an experience, and His ongoing ministry in the Church through the gifts. Faith, preaching, teaching, creeds, confessionals, expressive worship, ministration of the Holy Spirit, communion, water baptism, choreographed dancing, and dramatic presentations were skillfully integrated together with fixed liturgical elements. These were exciting times for me since it presented the opportunity for me to learn about the various dimensions of the Christian faith. Even more exciting to me was the Charismatic Mass we initiated as one of the three services offered on Sunday that provided for the corporate participation of the leaders and the congregation within a structured environment filled with both order and spontaneous celebration.

Because my religious background was not liturgical, it was most interesting when we replaced our traditional neckties and blouses for clerical collars. While liturgy and vestments had served as a boundary line between "high and low church traditions," this represented another effort to demonstrate a respect for historic forms while maintaining the power and ministration of the Holy Spirit. For me, it was a joy to get out of the neckties.

I discovered that this merging of form and power had its challenges. While form had an element of predictability and inspiration, power possessed a great degree of spontaneity, and the leadership constantly guarded against any competition between the ministry of the Holy Spirit and the order of the services. An order of service with a scheduled list of ministries such as songs, dances, dramatic presentations, announcements, and even the preaching of the Word was always subject to those unplanned events that were judged to be spiritually inspired. It demonstrated that freedom and order were compatible experiences. This was especially true for me since our chief musical director insisted on calling on me to sing a song without any prior notice. Often times during our services, when I least expected and had not rehearsed the words of the chosen song, she would beckon to me or simply start to play the introduction to the song. Those sounds would precipitate a high degree of anxiety within me. As much as I tried to ignore her, she would not be denied. In retrospect, I would laugh when I thought of those moments when Clarice Paulk, one of the founders and wife of Don Paulk, would turn my world upside down by just putting a note on that piano.

CHAPTER 5

THE WORD BECOMES FLESH

As previously mentioned, the local church had no outreach arm or any established network with other churches. The senior leadership was content to remain local until the proclamation and demonstration of the principles and power of the Kingdom of God gave visibility, credibility, and popularity to the ministry. There needed to be a strategy to serve the many ministries and churches that were being attracted to the teachings, music, dramatic presentations, and the various ministry programs of the church. Because of my interest in evangelism, Pastor Paulk assigned me the task of developing such a strategy, which I named "The Harvester Network of Churches," and it became a very effective avenue to teach and demonstrate the practical concepts of the Kingdom of God. Pastors and leaders from various denominations were attracted to the network, which provided a forum for the ongoing exchange of wisdom, counsel, and ministry resources. Its membership included leaders from within and outside the Pentecostal and Charismatic ranks. This was done in recognition of the unity and diversity in the Body of Christ. I was very enthusiastic about this phase of the ministry since it provided the opportunity for me to travel and experience the teachings and organizations of various churches. The network continued to thrive as an inclusive body of churches and ministries with membership throughout Africa, Asia, Australia, Europe, and South America.

While the network expanded, my philosophy of ministry was to simply serve as a liaison between the churches and the Cathedral. Bishop Paulk had specifically assigned me to keep him out of the daily operation of the network and to handle all ministry inquiries except those that needed his involvement. He did not desire to handle phone calls or accept the invitations to other churches, for this would keep him away from the Cathedral. In fact, he felt that the network was a form of "baby sitting the churches." Nevertheless, he trusted my judgment and accepted my constant recommendations. My popularity among the networks, however, posed an emotional threat of some kind. For example, during our annual conferences, the visiting pastors and leaders of ministries associated with our network would express their appreciation for my work among them. After all, it was my job to call them on a regular basis, address their concerns and connect them to the ministry resources at the Cathedral. Consequently, when they attended our network conferences, they would desire fellowship with me. Although I introduced them to Bishop Paulk and other members of our pastoral team, their desire to communicate with me during our conferences, posed a threat of some kind. As a result, the network was divided in section among some of our local pastors who did not necessarily have a vision nor a desire for such ministry. Nevertheless, it taught me a valuable lesson: Complaining compromises creativity. Therefore, rather than being upset by the change of structure, I took it as a good decision. This gave me the opportunity to develop a monthly video newsletter, which served as a vehicle to showcase the work of the Cathedral to an even wider audience.

Because the concept of the Kingdom presents the world as the field of ministry, the teachings, publications, music, and dramatic presentations of the Cathedral were exported to other states, countries, and nations. A most notable example of this exported influence was recorded in a newspaper article describing the impact of the ministry in South Africa. As aforementioned, Sandra and I were invited to South Africa to participate in the first inter-racial conference of the largest Pentecostal denomination. The churches in South Africa during the reign of apartheid ignored politics and simply preached the Gospel without stressing the ethical and moral demands of God upon government. Facing pressures from an emerging Liberation theology and Black liberals who demanded radical pronouncements and racial equality, the churches became confused and had no theology that could offer a viable solution. During one of our meetings with a large group of Bible students, a sudden anxiety entered the room as two young men dressed in black suits with ties came in unannounced. They sat quietly and listened attentively to my teaching. When the time of questions came around, one of them stood and read from a prepared document and they asked, "Was it Biblically appropriate to use violence to overthrow an ungodly government." As I carefully demonstrated the moral and ethical demands of the Kingdom of God, all in attendance were amazed as I presented the role of the church as a therapeutic community that is called to proclaim principles and demonstrates strategies of righteousness. I explained a theology of influence by which the church encourages government to enact laws and practices that honor Biblical principles. They had never heard that the church should be socially relevant and challenge ungodly world systems, so my answer gave them an alternative to violence.[9]

The message of the Kingdom of God was exciting to me because it made sense. In addition, it was practical, and it gave a sense of belonging to people who were not religious. As a result of the message of the Kingdom and the activities it precipitated, our local church received awards from President George H. Bush for its transforming work in the inner city public housing. Because the boundary line between the sacred and the secular was erased, socially active programs were designed and operated by volunteer teachers, entrepreneurs, doctors, nurses, athletes, and lawyers who established a resident ministry in one of the largest housing projects in Atlanta, Georgia. The influence of the church upon the lives of the residents and the social environment was so significant that the project captured the attention of the political community. At the height of its work and growth, the Cathedral was a model for many other churches in which entire communities were adopted as fields of ministry.

Since the message of the Kingdom is one of influence in society and communities, it openly validated the command of the Lord for Sandra and I to continue our dental practice. It must be remembered that from the beginning of our association with the church, there was a silent and open sentiment among some that we should resign dentistry. However, Bishop Paulk's understanding of the Kingdom and the encouragement of others gave us confirmation to do what we were committed to do.

CHAPTER 6

YE THAT ARE SPIRITUAL RESTORE

There is a proverbial saying that declares that where there is no ox then the stall is clean (Prov. 14:4). The implication is that where there are people, problems will exist. For that reason, the church is always a mixed company of the sick, well, living and the dying. The church as the incarnation of the Lord Jesus is a therapeutic community commissioned and endowed to restore those who are sick and have been ensnared with the challenges of life. Healing in all areas of sin is the work of the church, but we do not practice it. It must be understood, however, that restoration of confused and troubled people is risky business, and anyone involved in this redemptive process should expect challenges.

It must be remembered that Sandra and I maintained a part-time dental practice during our entire time at church. This provoked many questions and concern from people within and outside the walls of the church. Was it possible to do both? Did this compromise the idea of full-time ministry? After all, if I were a man of faith then, why did I need to depend upon dentistry? These questions and others almost provoked us to resign dentistry on three different occasions since the common view of full-time ministry demanded the desertion of any secular occupation. I am thankful to the Lord that three messengers were sent: Dr. Judson Cornwall, Archbishop Benson Idahosa and Bishop John Meares. Each of these men encouraged us to maintain our dental practice. In fact, the words of Dr. Cornwall still ring in my heart today. He said, "Dr. Clements, God has given you a foot in both worlds (secular and sacred)." Because of these three Divine interventions and the understanding of Bishop Paulk, we maintained our practice.

I discovered that challenges and questions are beneficial. They cause you to discover your motives. As the questions continued, my response was simply that whatever you love to do, you should do it well and without it being a burden. Colossians 3:23 states, "And whatsoever ye do, do it heartily, as to the Lord, and not unto men." I love people, and my desire is to help them. Moreover, I have never made a disconnection between ministry and dentistry. While the apostle Paul made tents, Dr. Clements made teeth! My dual role as a dentist and a pastor was an invaluable asset, for it greatly improved my approach to help people. For example, as a dentist, it was necessary to determine the nature and cause of the dental problems confronting my patients. The people whom I pastored had life problems. While pain looks the same, there are a variety of causes. For example, a patient could be suffering because of personal neglect due to ignorance or lack of finances. In some instances, dental care may not have been available for the patient. My role as a dentist was to make a proper assessment by examination of the problem and then prescribe a treatment that would be acceptable to the patient. This approach was the same in pastoral care. People suffer for a variety of reasons. Sometimes it is intentional or unintentional. The variable in the restoration process was always the patient and the member. That is, would they accept the treatment or counsel that was recommended, and would they follow my instructions? This connection between dentistry and ministry was invaluable and really influenced my approach in counseling.

My observations of the nature of ministry and where and how ministry takes place were recorded in a book titled *A Philosophy of Ministry*. This text included my understanding of the nature of the local church and the motivations behind the various ministries. For example, why did people join this ministry? Why did we establish certain social programs to help them? While the book explored topics relating to church, it enabled me to present a practical approach to help people resolve the conflicts and challenges in their lives. First of all, there was the necessity of making a proper diagnosis of the misbehavior including its cause, duration, and effect. Was the cause a character flaw, gullibility, or an expression of evil spirits? Second, what was the duration of the problem? Was the problem an initial occurrence or repeated offense? Third, what were the dimensions of the crisis? Was the crisis limited to the individual or did it involve others? Fourth, what is the response ability of the individual? Was the individual willing or able to follow the recommended steps for recovery? Of course, the confidentiality that was often necessary for the success of such a redemptive process could often be compromised by public exposure. Often times, confidentiality was the single most important factor, for it allowed the time to make correct judgment and decisions before the influx of public opinions.

A critical factor in the ministry of the Cathedral was the desire of its leader, Archbishop Earl Paulk, to protect anointings and to restore people. I strongly respected this character trait in him and personally sat in his company as he ministered life and restoration to some of the most challenging and hopeless circumstances. When one of the most public figures in Christian television was imprisoned, Earl Paulk stood with him. When the public television ministry of Jim Bakker came to a tragic end, Earl Paulk publically endorsed the good works of that ministry. At the death of Archbishop Benson Idahosa of Nigeria and the possible fragmentation and disintegration of a ministry that transformed nations for Jesus Christ, it was the boldness of Archbishop Earl Paulk to travel to Nigeria, set things in order, and then ordain Dr. Margaret Idahosa as the bishop in that ministry. I was privileged to travel with him and to witness the entire process. In fact, my present involvement and influence in the Idahosa ministry is due in part to the legacy established by Archbishop Paulk during those most trying times. All of these experiences greatly influenced my philosophy of ministry.

Since Jesus came to "seek and save that which was lost" (Luke 19:10), and "the sick have need of a physician and not the well" (Matt. 9:12), the Cathedral stood as a place of restoration for the oppressed, the estranged, the devalued, the misfits, the fallen, and all who had come short of the glory of God or who existed outside of the boundaries of social and cultural norms. Agin, the first message preached in the newly constructed Cathedral was titled: Whosoever Will, Let Them Come.

The Cathedral was endowed with the gifts and callings necessary to discern, counsel, and mentor those who presented themselves and their problems. There were elders with keen discernment, pastoral instinct, and prophetic insights. Most importantly, there was the ministry of the congregation that had been conditioned through all of our teachings to be sensitive to those who were in need of care in the congregation. In essence, restoration was a corporate responsibility of both the leadership and the congregation. This concept influenced other churches in their dealing with the challenges of their congregations.

As the years passed, I began to understand the comprehensive nature of the salvation process. Salvation is spiritual, psychological, and behavioral. The spiritual involves the Divine/human connection and the finished work of Christ Jesus. We are delivered from the power of evil and put into a new kingdom. The psychological is the transformation of our minds with ideas, thoughts, values, and objectives. While our minds are empowered to receive truth, we must study and embrace the wonderful benefits of this great salvation. And the behavioral aspect of salvation is our human response in attitude and practice to such truth. For example, the apostle Paul reminds the Colossians that they have been delivered from the power of darkness and have been translated into the kingdom Christ Jesus (Col.1:13). The apostle Paul also encourages them not to be in subjection to commandments and doctrines of men that take away their liberty in Christ Jesus (Col. 2:20-22). We can be free and yet still behave as slaves!

As the local ministry expanded, my trans-local ministry increased tremendously. I was often invited to speak at churches and conferences both nationally and internationally. This was a great joy to me, for I felt the greatest level of productivity and personal satisfaction when I ministered in different environments. The Cathedral was a highly respected model for me to display. I often spoke of our different ministries, especially the social programs. One of our ministry philosophies was to offer solutions rather than complaints. In that sense, the church became a cultural architect and not a cultural critic. Architects create beautiful things from ideas and thoughts. Critics can be guilty of finding faults without offering solutions.

This was particularly true regarding the abortion issue. It was a very explosive topic and often the pro-life and pro-choice factions were at odds. On one of my visit to a network church, the host pastor took me to a protest rally where a crowd had surrounded an abortion clinic. I will never forget the impact of that scene upon my mind. There were news reporters and police officers and an angry crowd of protesters. The crowd stalked the clinic, and its anger was contagious. When we left the protest meeting, I discovered that the pastor was one of the organizers. As we talked about the events of that day, I asked him about his ministry for the young women who got pregnant out of wedlock. I also asked him if any alternatives beside abortion, were offered to them. He described the theological and social implications of the abortion issue, but he offered no viable alternative. The women who visited that clinic were challenged to feel guilty and ashamed, but there were no alternatives offered to them beyond the condemnation.

At our local church, we cooperated with an adoption agency to facilitate the adoption of babies born out of wedlock. The compassion of our congregation was unbelievable. If you could only witness the liturgy of adoption in a hospital room, it would move you to tears. Around the bed that housed the mother and the newborn would be adoptive parents and a pastor, and with prayer and proper documentation, the transfer of a life was presented to new parents. That was a compassionate and powerful solution!

We also formed a ministry to help those individuals who were struggling with any form of addiction. It was appropriately called The Overcomers Ministry. Counsel, and it provided for the restoration of people and leaders who experienced personal challenges and failures. Small groups would meet in different rooms of the church under the direction of seasoned elders and workers. Unlike other agencies of recovery, we did not believe that one would always be an addict simply because he or she was once addicted. Whom the Son has set free is free indeed (John 8:36). That freedom comes with a new identity. I spoke at many of the gatherings of that ministry that met every Monday night at 7 p.m. My heart would leap as I listened to the testimonies of people who were in various stages of deliverance and healing. Restorative compassion was definitely alive! Because of such efforts, many more productive citizens are in the Kingdom of God today.

A significant principle in the philosophy of ministry of the Cathedral was the distinction between the ideal and the exception. Creation established the ideal of Divine purposes, intentions, and functions, while sin initiated the perversion or the exception to this ideal. Humanity was made in the image of God and was not constituted to sin, which is a contradiction to human nature. Consequently, there was a consistent effort to preach and demonstrate the ideal for a contemporary world of people, institutions, organizations, governments, and laws, while ministering to the very individuals and systems that fell short of that ideal. This concept was a challenge to those who could only see their mistakes or failures. Faith looks beyond the obvious. It is not a denial of reality, rather, it is the recognition of finality. Irrevocable norms, values, and practices are acceptable in any culture. However, there are also exceptions to these standards. For example, freedom, love, justice, equity, and peace may be ideals, while oppression, hatred, injustice, discrimination, and war are exceptions. The Gospel is the declaration of the purposes and intentions of God for humanity and all creation. It is amazing what happens when alternatives and possibilities are set before people. It is said of the Lord Jesus that He endured the contradiction of sinners because of the joy that was set before Him. Thus, we firmly believe that when that which is set before us is greater than that which is around us, then we can develop the will to pursue the greater. The Church is the representative of the consciousness of these Divine ideals.

As previously mentioned, the Church is the therapeutic community where healing, deliverance, inspiration, reconciliation, and restoration occur. Each day, I could see the redemptive products of this ministry; I could also recognize the process. That is, the congregation of the Cathedral was always a mixture of the well, the sick, the rich, the poor, the mature, and the immature. It was the place where the ideal was preached and ministry was provided to the exception. It was a place where all were welcome.

I must admit that of all the things learned, that the compassion of the Lord Jesus was most powerful. He was moved with compassion when He saw people scattered without shepherds (Matt. 9:36). People are possibilities waiting for the influence of the Word and the Spirit upon their minds and hearts. Since the Kingdom of God is righteousness, joy and peace in the Holy Ghost (Rom. 14:17), then it is the compassionate Kingdom. It is the rebranding of people and the world. May the spiritual continue to restore!

CHAPTER 7

COMMUNITY OF THE HOLY GHOST

Perhaps the most powerful aspect of this journey was the dynamic of the Holy Spirit. We learned that the presence of the Holy Spirit in our lives was no substitute for sound minds and sound beliefs. We receive the Holy Spirit as power and not as intelligence. The Holy Spirit is the power of God, while the Scripture contains the intelligence. You can have the Holy Spirit power and still lack Scriptural intelligence. Since the person and ministry of the Holy Spirit is integral to the Kingdom of God, something is to be said about the doctrine of the Holy Spirit as an experience of real power (Rom. 14:17). This is most significant in our discussion since the church, known as Chapel Hill Harvester, became identified as the Cathedral of the Holy Spirit. A brief review of Church history reveals the separation of the principle and practice of the Holy Spirit.

Historically, the primitive Church was a charismatic community in which the Holy Spirit was the executive agent who administrated all things pertaining to the Church (John 16:7-11; 1 Cor. 12; Eph. 2:17-23, 4:3-7). In fact, it was the Holy Spirit who validated the ministry of the Church (Mark

16:15-18; Acts 15:6-8), and gave witness to the resurrection (Acts 2:32-33, 4:33); commissioned ministers (Acts 1:4-8, 6:3-5, 13:1-4; Rom. 10:15; 1 Tim. 1:18, 4:14); facilitated evangelism (Acts 8:5-17, 29-38, 10:1-48); directed ministry (Acts 10:19-20, 44-47, 16:6-10); administered judgments (Acts 5:1-11, 15:6-11); adjusted prejudice (Acts 11:12-17); and gave prophetic warnings (Acts 11:27-28, 21:10-11). It was the Holy Spirit at work within the fixed liturgical structures that gave productive life to the corporate gathering of the Church community. We experienced this at the Cathedral as we explored the fixed world of liturgy and structure. We made sure that we did not lose the energy, creativity, and liberty of the Holy Spirit in the process of designing Sunday morning programs.

With the death of the early apostles and disciples, the Holy Spirit became less the object of experience and more the object of faith. The rise of false teachers and the infiltration of the Church with strange doctrines and heresies provided the need to reconsolidate the Church around some central authority and doctrine. In the late first and second centuries, there was an increasing concern for the details of rules, rights, and dogmas.[10] There was a corresponding decline of the interest in the relationship of the Church and the Holy Spirit.

Even though the primitive Church was almost exclusively a charismatic community with the Holy Spirit taking form in the "one Body of the exalted Christ," gradually, the Holy Spirit was replaced with liturgical structures and other substitutes.[11] Direct inspiration of the Spirit became suspect. Since water baptism was regulated and faith and Spirit inspiration were not, the Spirit became more confined to the Church in Catholicism. Eventually, the Spirit became the possession of the Church and was associated with ritual acts. The bishop alone was authorized to bestow the Spirit.

The Protestant reaction to this ritualism and sacramental theology was to be seen in its emphasis in preaching and personal faith.[12] Authority was to be centered in the Bible and not in the Church. Faith was emphasized as being distinct and necessary prior to water baptism, and water baptism was subordinated to faith and the role of preaching. The Holy Spirit was viewed as the initiator of faith. Even though the activities of the Holy Spirit during the apostolic age were readily acknowledged, the Protestants assumed the position that the "charismata" ceased with the apostles. The Spirit became subordinate to the Scripture and the Scripture took the place of the Catholic sacraments as the significant means of grace and inspiration. While the Catholics focused on the objectivity of the sacraments, the Protestants focused on the objectivity of the Scriptures.

The Pentecostals were against the rituals and sacramental emphasis of the Catholics and the intellectual orthodoxy of the Protestants. Subsequently, they focused their attention on the experience of the Holy Spirit. The Baptism in the Holy Spirit and the gifts of the Spirit are justified in the New Testament as being legitimate experiences in the lives of the early Christians (Acts 2:4; 4:31; 9:31; 10:44-46; 13:52; 19:6; Rom. 5:5; 8:1-16; I Cor. 12:7,13; II Cor. 3:6; 5:5; Gal. 4:6; 5:16-18, 25; I Thess. 1:5; Titus 3:6; John 3:8; 4:14; 7:38; 16:7). However, the Pentecostals separated the Spirit-baptism from the event of conversion-initiation and made the gift of the Spirit an experience, which followed after conversion. According to Paul and Luke, the Spirit is not something given subsequent to and distinct from becoming a Christian, nor is the Spirit only bestowed by an apostle or a bishop, or simply an experience restricted to the apostolic days.

Although the theological roots of The Cathedral of the Holy Spirit were in classical Pentecostalism, the Baptism of the Holy Spirit was viewed as an integral part of the conversion-initiation experience. As aforementioned, deliberate efforts were taken to demonstrate that the preaching of the Word and the administration of the sacraments of the Eucharist and water baptism were not competing elements. The manifestation of the Holy Spirit in and through theologically informed saints was the welcomed and expected dimension of the corporate worship gathering. Furthermore, the administration of the baptism of the Holy Spirit as a present day phenomenon is also a responsibility of the priesthood of the believers. The believers and the leaders can "lay hands on" (Mark 16:18; Acts 13:3; 2 Tim. 1:6) and facilitate the baptism of the Holy Spirit, healing, and deliverance.

During the years of our travel and experience with churches, we saw a subtle anti-Charismatic sentiment creep into many of the ministries. Where many of the churches had experienced the freedom, creativity and spontaneity of the Holy Spirit, there was a gradual decline in preaching that was sprinkled with words of knowledge, wisdom and prophecies. Intellectuality became a substitute for spirituality. The gatherings of the redeemed communities became more like a spectator sport where the entertainers performed on stage and the congregation simply watched. The congregations gathered with their notebooks to glean information. Their heads were informed, but their spirits were not always touched.

We struggled with this at the Cathedral. As the ministry

became more visible and popular, it attracted all kinds of people. There were political and social dignitaries who often attended the meetings, and it was not uncommon for national and international leaders to be present. There were times when we were impressed with their presence, so we desired to present our most polished programs with all of its theatric drama and tapestry. Therefore, there was always the challenge of maintaining a tension between the dynamic of the Holy Spirit and the fixed liturgy of dramatic presentations and musical programs. We maintained the balance and always remained open to the gentle moving of the Holy Spirit. After all, the thing that attracted the crowds in the beginning was the power of the Spirit and the message of the Kingdom.

CHAPTER 8

TABERNACLE MADE WITH HANDS

During years as a pastor, I moved from one kind of building to another. As previously noted, we once worshipped the Lord in a large circus tent for over a year. During the winter, neither blankets nor gigantic space heaters could solve my dilemma. For me, that was the coldest weather in the history of the South. That said, I firmly believe that heaven is warm and hell is cold.

While we never lost track of the idea that the people are the church and not a place nor a building, we did experience a convergence of theology and construction. While Pentecostals were accustomed to a theology of escape from this present world, there was rarely any emphasis on building a tabernacle of any permanence. Although the concepts of the Kingdom of God became the catalyst for a new kind of construction with a definite degree of permanence, resident in the local church ministry were architects, builders, engineers, and visionaries. When all of these ingredients intersected with strong prophetic ministers, the result was the first neo-gothic Cathedral built by a classical Pentecostal body of believers. This was a most exciting phase of the journey, so a little history is needed.

I was often called upon to dedicate a home, building, and even a church facility. It is interesting to note that most of my Scriptural references at that time were taken from the Old Testament. In the New Testament, the Lord Jesus spoke of tearing down buildings or He made reference to the tabernacle of His body (Matt. 27:40; Mark 14:58; John 2:19-22). Historically, it is written that the Holy Spirit does not dwell in "temples made with hands" (Acts 17:24). A scan of history of the Christian Church shows that worship took place in catacombs, fields, in homes, by the river, in prisons, on ships, in automobiles, and even in airplanes. However, it was normal for believers to have a set place of worship.[13] These places of worship communicated something about the conviction of the people. For what we do in worship is expressed in the design and use of the building space. As aforementioned, this principle was demonstrated in the physical structure of the Cathedral.[14] The neo-gothic exterior with its interior choir lofts, baptismal founts, stained glass windows, padded pews, and all of the tapestries were an expression of the "liturgical" elements and an integration of the old and the new. In addition to the physical structures, there was the experience of the melodies and the songs of historic hymns, the contemporary gospels, the classical melodies, and spiritual songs all being delivered through choirs, special groups, and a full-scale orchestra. There was choreographed dancing by trained and talented artisans coupled with the spontaneous celebration of praise and worship among the congregation. Also, there was the Spirit dynamic of prophecy, tongues and interpretation, miracles, healings, and all the other ministration of the gifts of the Holy Spirit.

We demonstrated a "convergent theology," which influenced

the attitude and behavior of the local church toward worship. It was a synthesis of the essentials of the Christian faith, both in theory and practice. In essence, we demonstrated an integration of the contributions of the diverse branches of the faith such as the Orthodox tradition, with its liturgical and sacramental emphasis; the Reformed tradition, with its emphasis on the centrality of Scriptures, justification by faith and the universal priesthood; the Pentecostal tradition, with its emphasis on the Baptism of the Holy Spirit and its diverse ministration. We also integrated the various polarities of the Kingdom of God into a system of practical and applied theology that provided outlets for the demonstrations of its concepts (Rom. 14:17; 1 Cor. 15:24, 50; Gal. 5:21; Eph. 5:5; Col.1:13; 4:11; 2 Thess. 1:5).

I remember our first meeting in the newly constructed Cathedral. It was filled to capacity. Political and social dignitaries were present. What an exciting day it was as testimonials and proclamations were in an abundance from our pastors and the people. I offered the congregational prayer that morning, and Bishop Paulk preached a powerful message entitled, *Whosoever Will Let Him Come*. As I listened and observed all of the activities, I could feel a very subtle interaction at work. The people had been accustomed to worshipping in different tabernacles that were not as grand as this one, so the vastness and grandeur of this "tabernacle which was made with hands," commanded their attention. To me, it stifled their worship of the Lord. I remember making a few statements as I led the congregation in prayer. I said that while this building is new and beautiful, we should not let it hinder our expressions of praise to the Lord. I even remember likening the Cathedral to an overgrown pine arbor. The people from southern Georgia understood my reference for the Bishop would often make reference to his father preaching in the country under a hand-made canopy of freshly cut pine branches. I remember how that comment brought some spiritual reality into the room, and it even made me even more conscious of the need to maintain a delicate balance in ministry.

God still imparted principles and models of righteousness through the Church that needed to be proclaimed and demonstrated in the midst of a fragmented and confused world.

CHAPTER 9

CONTROVERSY, CONTRADICTION AND CRISIS

This is the part of the journey that we would have desired to avoid. Perhaps we were forewarned by a dream that Sandra shared with me before all of the events occurred. She dreamed of a great flood of water rushing through and around all the buildings of the Cathedral property, and it even included the houses around the surrounding community. The water did not destroy the buildings nor the houses, but it flushed out all of the debris and trash that was hidden around and under them. We discussed the dream and its meaning and concluded that the meaning was not literal but symbolic. The water represented the Holy Spirit or even a judgment while the buildings and houses were symbolic of ministries, people and even lifestyles. The debris and trash spoke of anything that was contaminated, unclean, and undesired. Sandra shared the dream with Bishop Paulk, and he acknowledged that it was prophetic. Our journey was about to carry us through a period where things that were once hidden and silent were about to be revealed and shouted from the roof top. A major crisis was, no doubt, at hand.

We had labored for over two years to complete the

construction of a beautiful neo-gothic cathedral with all of its stained-glass windows, padded pews, baptismal font, choir loafs, nursery rooms, and the hallways that completely circled the entire worship space. It would be the first of its kind constructed by a group of Pentecostals. I was thrilled with the prospect since we had gone through a series of tabernacles made with hands. We had moved from the original building where the ministry expanded into a large circus tent; surprisingly, the congregation grew during the hottest summer and the coldest winter. From the tent, we had moved to a newly constructed "airplane hanger" called appropriately the 'K-Center." We had also constructed a large multi-purpose building adjacent to this structure. Our crowning achievement would be the completion of the cathedral, for we had planned a conference that would attract nations and the most notable speakers in the Pentecostal and Charismatic circles. Despite all of our plans and labor, however, we were not able to complete the cathedral before the conference. So, all the meetings were held in the K-Center.

The 1990 World Conference on the Kingdom of God was exciting. Leaders from over 80 nations and a massive crowd, including our own growing congregation, attended this festive event that lasted for an entire week. The campus was covered with small tents that housed the food and product vendors. It was an experience that exceeded anything we had imagined. I had been a vital part of the planning because of my role overseeing the many churches associated with our ministry. During the conference, I was given the responsibility of giving the speakers the time, and duration of their teaching assignments. I also had the privilege to personally transport some of the speakers back and forth from their hotels to the conference area. Although, the days and nights seemed endless, there was an energy and an enthusiasm that made them appear as a breath of a moment. From all assessment by the guests and the local people, the conference was a tremendous success.

After this exciting and meaningful conference, allegations of sexual immorality among some of the key leadership, staff and members of the congregation, flared up. As a member presbytery, I was told by the senior leaders of the possibilities that accusations would be made evident. The accusers were "demonized," and they were labored as the enemies of God, by the senior leadership, As pastors, to heightened the scandal, we were strongly advised to disbelieve the reports of sexual immorality among some of the key senior leaders and staff members. It was shocking and disappointing to me that certain accusations were being made. Even though there were possibilities that some of these accusations could be true, there was the source of tremendous emotional conflicts in my mind.

The scandal was publicized locally, nationally, and internationally. As you can imagine, there were threats and lawsuits against key leaders. I remember how the four founding leaders came to our home with copies of legal documents that had been issued against them and the church. I presented the documents to our Law Guild, which was a group of all the attorneys who were members of the church. Our son was an attorney, and our daughter would become an attorney a few years later. The Guild would meet monthly in our home after a Sunday service for fellowship. At this crucial time, they became a resource of counsel for those leaders who were accused.

The effect upon the local church was devastating. Several leaders and hundreds of members abandoned the ministry, so the economic foundation plunged to an all-time low. The nature of the scandal persisted throughout the 1990s and into the new millennium. There appeared to be a cycle of allegations and exposures that shook the ministry. After each crisis, there were periods of recovery, restoration, and re-certification.

Since the scandals had now become public record, the public had questions and wanted answers. Many of our members and leaders were receiving phone calls from different news agencies and churches. Our presbytery decided to centralize the communication process between the Cathedral and the news agencies. Since my role required me to travel extensively to other churches, ministries and conferences, I was assigned to serve as the official liaison between the Cathedral and the media. The local, national and international media converged upon the Cathedral and even camped outside during regular worship services to get interviews and photographs. There were times when news reporters even sat among the congregation and gathered in the hallways in hope of getting an interview with members or leaders as they entered or exited the buildings during the worship services. At times, the atmosphere outside the walls of the Cathedral had news vans and marked cars parked along the public streets. Our ushers did an outstanding job in managing the disruptions.

At the root of the scandals, there was suspect of a doctrine among a small minority of senior leaders that provided for the justification and "covering" of the sexual immorality. This suspicion was confirmed when a young married couple came to Sandra and I for counsel. The wife was pregnant and in great distress for her husband had confessed his infidelity with a staff member of the church. This extra-marriage relationship began as a casual friendship and evolved into a more serious matter. The young man and the staff member sought counsel with a senior leader who condoned the relationship. Sandra and I strongly upbraided him for his infidelity and failure to assume responsibility for his immorality. Some of these individuals so desired to be accepted by certain leaders that they were willing to sacrifice their personal integrity. There were others who desired to engage in such promiscuity and only needed some approval or alleged license from someone to pursue their desires. Such reports seemed to affirm some of the allegations. However, the senior leaders continued to deny the reports. It was shocking and disappointing.

The doctrine that I mentioned is referred to as "covering" and is a concept taken from Genesis 3:21 whereby the Lord provides animal skins to conceal the nakedness of Adam and Eve after their transgression. In a contemporary context, it can mean to create a therapeutic environment through counseling, deliverance, repentance and confidentiality that allows for the restoration and recovery of the individual. While the idea of covering was initially introduced in Genesis in its association with sin, it was later expanded by various theologians to include governmental supervision over individuals and even groups. This idea of covering was viewed as the function of elders and included daily ministry of caring for the congregation (Heb. 13:7,17).

However, let it be said that covering is not a system for the justification of any misbehavior; rather, it is supposed to represent the care of another. Unfortunately, there are times when the abuse or misuse of a Biblical principle or precept generates a skepticism and even a disdain of its further use. For example, the Discipleship Movement emphasized ministerial and personal accountability for decision, judgment, and behavior. However, the extreme administration of the principles of accountability by some of the leaders resulted in skepticism and even disdain for such structure in succeeding generations of church leaders. The correction of abuse was not the discontinuation of a practice or principle; it was the proper use.

The government of the Cathedral consisted of a corporate group of local elders called presbyters. In addition to this body of leaders, there existed a group of leaders outside of the church who were supposed to be the covering of the local elders, especially the senior leaders. This system of covering only works effectively where there is honesty, trust, and communication among those covered and those providing the covering. While the outside elders could be willing and be able to provide the covering, the system is ineffective when the local elders lack integrity and fail to reveal the truth.

At the Cathedral, it became obvious that the sexual immorality was restricted to a few individuals. As previously stated, there was a philosophy of managing misbehavior at the eldership level. It involved elders who administered the process of restoration and recovery after a transgression (Gal. 6:1). That is, when someone sinned, he or she had to make a confession to an elder or someone "over him or her in the Lord." The individual had to demonstrate a heart of repentance and genuine change. The judgment or absolution for the transgression could be dismissal or excommunication from the ministry for a period of time. The sentence, when necessary, could demand private or public confession, and the continuation of ministry in some form of work done away from the city or town where the transgression occurred.

Because covering occurred when confession was made "upward" or to someone who was "over you in the Lord," then it was alleged that there was no need to confess "down" to anyone else including a local presbytery nor the people. In fact, after confession and absolution, there could be a denial that any sin or mistake occurred since the Scripture admonishes us to forget the things that are past and to make no reference to the unfruitful works of darkness (Phil. 3:13; Eph. 5:11). For this reason, an individual could assume ministry with confidence that forgiveness had been granted when there was true repentance.

During our travel among the network of churches that were related to the Cathedral, Sandra and I were often asked about the allegations. In fact, during one our ministry trips, a group of over fifty pastors asked to meet with us to discuss the nature and dimension of the scandals. They desired to know the complete nature of the scandals, the people involved, and how the matters were being managed. I felt that their questions and concerns were genuine, and many offered to pray for the ministry. We attempted to be as honest and informative as possible. Even though we had personally received reports from some individuals that seemed to justify the allegations, the accused leaders had not acknowledged any guilt.

These were very challenging times as we travelled among the network of churches and even attended conferences, for just as we were once accepted because of our association with the Cathedral, we were now estranged and even criticized because of the same association. In fact, a very popular Christian magazine had featured the scandal with photographs of the Cathedral. The article also featured a photograph of a news conference at the Cathedral where Bishop Paulk, our attorney, and I were seated on a stage as we made some official statements. The Bishop had asked me to sit with them. This magazine was circulated during a major conference that Sandra and I attended annually. As a result of the photographs, some of the organizers and leaders of the conference separated themselves from us. They had accused us by reason of association.

These were, no doubt, trying times, and the numerous phones calls and inquiries were endless. Because of my role with the network of churches and as the official liaison between the church and the media, it was emotionally taxing. Since the scandal was so publicized, I even felt constrained to make some mention of the issue whenever I was invited to speak at a church or conference.

Sandra and I received comfort as we reflected on the dream of the great flood of water flushing out all the debris from around and under the building and some of the houses in the communities. In the dream, there was no destruction of the building or the houses. In retrospect, this indicated a time of recovery. Indeed, after each scandal, there was a period of restoration of the credibility, popularity, and productivity of the ministry. There was never any confession of guilt, and most troubling was the lack of repentance.

The last scandal received the greatest notoriety. The individuals accused of the transgression claimed their innocence and those making the claims were accused of slander. However, the credibility of the accusations could not be dismissed because of the status of those who initiated the claims. They were individuals who were leaders or former leaders at the Cathedral. The unwillingness or inability of those accused to repent may have indicated a great degree of self-deception and a misapplication of the concept of covering. It must be remembered that the effectiveness of any system of recovery and restoration is dependent upon integrity and true repentance. It would later be proven that both integrity and repentance were lacking.

During those very challenging times, there were guest ministers who came and preached in our services. However, if they had made any reference to the scandals or the need for repentance, they would not be invited back again. Beside the Bishop, I was often assigned to minister in the services. My messages were pastoral and prophetic in nature since they would often cite the work of the Lord among us as a people and then project the possibility of promises to be fulfilled. My words would encourage and comfort the people because the Lord had given me credibility among the leaders and the congregation. There were prophetic words spoken through me regarding the restoration and recovery of the ministry that had come to pass. My prophetic words had constrained the senior leaders from abandoning some critical aspects of the ministry such as television outreach. There had been times when decisions had been made not to renew contracts with certain Christian television networks because the cost was not justified by the fruit. My words would always remind the leaders that we were a mission-oriented church called to demonstrate and proclaim the truths and power of the Kingdom of God. Furthermore, the value of ministry should not be determined by the income it generates. For these and other reasons, the credibility of my words were accepted and acted upon.

Those phases of the Cathedral were most critical since they shaped the internal climate of the ministry and conditioned the external reactions and responses from the public. While the crisis was seemingly described as human misbehavior, carnality, and lawlessness, there were a host of other factors involved. For example, a number of contributing factors such as religious traditions and doctrinal confusion existed. A critical principle that I observed was that spiritual entities masqueraded themselves in natural ways. That is, internal convictions, whether correct or incorrect, are ultimately expressed in some form of operational behavior. This was a major concern to me since I desired to know the reasons and the beliefs behind these conflicts.

My practice of dentistry provided me a most beneficial concept during the scandals. For example, when patients came to my office in pain, it was necessary for me to make a proper diagnosis before starting with a treatment. Without knowing the cause and nature of their dental problems, no treatment was rendered. The ministry was no exception. I was convinced that the root causes had to be discovered. This line of thinking proved to be invaluable to me during those very difficult times. Since there was no acknowledgment of guilt nor repentance and the credibility of the accusations were growing beyond measure, I desired to know the total nature of this crisis. I knew that Sandra and I would have to provide answers in the years to come.

CHAPTER 10

RELIGIOUS TRADITIONS

Traditions are defined as long standing beliefs and convictions that influence attitudes and patterns of behavior. Historically, the battleground of the universal Church has always been doctrinal and theological. That is, the struggle has resided in human efforts to interpret the Biblical truths and put them into a manageable and practical form. This challenge has expressed itself in mixture or the addition of non-Biblical elements (Gal. 1:6-9; 3:1; 5:13-25; Col. 1-2; 1 Thes. 5:19-22). It has also presented itself in the form of overspecialization or the overemphasis of certain aspects of the salvation experience at the expense of some very fundamental elements (1 Thes. 4:13-18; 2 Thes. 2:1-15; Acts 20:27; 1 Cor. 15:12-58). This challenge has often emerged in the distortion of Biblical principles and precepts such as faith, spiritual authority, deliverance, divine healing and even gender (Rom. 3:1-8; 21-31; 1Cor. 11:2-16, 19; 14:34-35; Gal. 2:16; 3:1-14, 28; 6:15; Eph. 5:21-33; Col. 3:11; Heb. 8; Jam. 5:13-16). Let's examine some of these.

Faith represents our contractual relationship with God and is the medium of this Divine/human relationship. In some circles, faith was assumed to demand a denial of reality in which the believer confessed that problems such as sickness, disease, or financial deficiencies did not exist even though they may have been present (Phil. 4:8; Rom.10:10; Heb. 11:1-40). This practice was supposed to be an emulation of Abraham, the father of faith, who called those things "that be not" as though they were (Rom. 4:17). However, Sandra and I have witnessed individuals who denied medical assistance because their internal faith propositions caused them to disbelieve the symptoms or any evidence of disease. Fortunately, for us, we merged faith and medicine and sought proper treatment for health challenges that faced us.

While there is some truth in the principle, faith is not a denial of reality but the recognition of finality. It is not necessary to deny the existence of problems or challenges to have faith. However, I discovered that belief does demand a certain degree of disbelief. That is, I can acknowledge the presence of a problem, but I must believe that God has the last word on the situation. By faith, we recognize the sovereignty of God over times, seasons, and circumstances (Rom. 13:1). By faith we recognize that God has the last word in every situation (Prov. 21:30). Consequently, by faith, we accept the coexistence of a world that is seen and one that is unseen (Rom. 1:20; Heb. 6:5). The things that are obvious appear in the seen or natural world while the power, promise, privileges, and provisions reside in the unseen or spiritual word. By confession and obedience, the believer accesses the unseen world with its wonderful possibilities and promises (Rom. 10:9-10). However, it is not confession alone, for it is difficult to resolve by confession what behavior has caused (Rom. 12:1-2; Heb. 12:1; Jam. 2:14-26).

Now, this concept of faith enabled us to accept the reality

of the problems at the Cathedral while recognizing the Divine promise. We were not in denial, for the problems were real, and confession alone was not going to remove them. Without repentance, all human efforts of recovery would end in hypocrisy.

I wanted to discover the misconception of the faith principle, and it appeared in the concept of law. The term *antinomianism* means "against the law." It is the belief that one can live outside the boundaries of regulations and laws of society (1 Cor. 5:1). From a theological perspective, *antinomianism* is the belief that faith alone, not moral law, is necessary for salvation. So, the antinomian attempts to live above the law or social restrictions because of some faith, grace, or knowledge that grant special freedom.

Christianity, however, has always recognized that justification by faith does not deny the restraints of moral law. The Corinthian epistle is an example of the Apostle Paul's effort to maintain a proper tension between faith and moral law in the lives of people (1 Cor. 5:1-13; 6:1-20; 7:1-5). An antinomian is one who attempts to justify any moral perversion by pleading the power of faith alone (Jam. 1:21-27; 2:14-26). For example, in some of our presbytery meetings, the senior leader would say that he was taught by his father that if his mother disciplined his siblings incorrectly, that she was right even if she were wrong. This concept must have entered into Bishop Paulk's ministry philosophy for I heard him say many times that if he were wrong regarding his ministry, then he would still be right because only God could judge him. A proper tension, nevertheless, must exist between the instructive value of Biblically revealed moral law and the power of faith in the life of the believer (1 Cor. 9:19-21). Without some universal guidelines and landmarks to direct the ethical and moral course, then every person is left to do that which seems right in his/her own sight, like in the dark ages. Judges 21:25 reflects such a state: "In those days there was no king in Israel; every man did that which was right in his own eyes." The logical progression of such thinking is "situational ethics" from which judgment originated the "force of the moment" rather than from the gravitational influences of a historic law. I recognize the extreme of legalism in the opposite direction where a law never takes into consideration other contributing factors or circumstances. The antinomian, however, does not recognize any historic norm or has been conditioned by a false historic norm.

There were times during our Presbytery meetings when the senior leader would make statements that provoked concern. For example, he was known to say that only God could judge him and that the Lord knew what he needed. While those in attendance may not have accepted this and other similar statements, no one would respond nor challenge such statements. If someone ventured to disagree with the status quo, that individual would either be ignored or accused indirectly of being an Absalom or Judas.

We had received such strong teachings on spiritual authority and respect for leadership. Even though the members of the presbytery were leaders themselves, they had witnessed and even experienced the consequences of violating the status quo. They could either be ignored or indirectly be labeled as an Absalom or a Judas. I discovered that if a person had a conviction about any topic, the person had to be prepared to accept the consequences of making that known. I believe, in retrospect, that such an environment made leaders either stronger or weaker. It also forced us, as leaders, to discern the spiritual and psychological climate of a meeting and to carefully choose the appropriate time and nature of our responses.

Strong leaders are usually dominant and very opinionated, and those who work alongside such strong leaders must understand that it is more effective if an individual met privately with such leaders rather than confronted them publicly. I did not consider it wise nor profitable to challenge a leader publicly. Some issues are best handled privately. I firmly believe that one could express his or her conviction if it were done in a spirit of love, cooperation, and kindness. However, if a person chose to violate his or her personal integrity through silence and dishonesty with him or herself, the psychological consequences could be destructive. Depression, despair, sadness, and other negative emotional signs will manifest themselves. For example, I had a dream during the early phases of this last scandal that addressed this premise regarding suppressed anger and guilt. The dream revealed the depth of my own pain and despair. In the dream, I was in a very deep underground cave with some of my fellow presbyters. It was dark, but I could discern the voices and faces of those present. They were so despondent and angry because of their emotional pain caused by criticism leveled against them by the senior leader that they were willing to set fire to the dungeon. In the dream, their pain had caused them to become self-destructive. I cautioned them not to be destructive, but they still set fire to the dungeon because of their emotional pain. On one of the walls of the dungeon, there was a light that seemed to shine down from above through a stairwell that led out of the dungeon. I moved toward the light while some sought to hinder me. Nevertheless, I managed to walk up the long flight of stairs. As I walked up the stairs, one of the leaders came behind me to stop me from leaving. When we exited the top of the stairs, we were outside and in the light. At the point, I realized the depth of the dungeon.

Symbolically, the dream revealed the depth of the despair that resided in the hearts of us all because of the scandal and the suppression of truth. The despair was so intense that some were exhibiting self-destructive behavioral patterns such as self-doubt, resentment, anxiety and anger. In the dream, when I left the group, the members did not desire me to leave because of the fear that their status would be revealed. All of the presbyters were not in the dream.

I later revealed the dream to our Presbytery but not to the senior leaders. I remember how many of them responded to the dream and its meaning. One even commented that there was no place for truth in that ministry because of the consequences. However, we all shared our pain and concern among ourselves at that meeting. The criticism and guilt manipulation was prevalent from the pulpit during the scandals. Many times, the pastors were blamed for the declining crowds. They were also accused of not shepherding the people properly. However, the cause of the declining ministry was not the pastors, rather, it was the manner in which the crisis was handled from the pulpit by the senior leaders. The constant denunciation and demonizing of the accusers and those who were leaving the ministry were not edifying. Moreover, the self- exoneration from any guilt and the blaming of others did not create a healthy spiritual and psychological climate.

It became obvious to me, that the best strategy to express personal opinions and views in our presbytery meetings was to put them in a non-confrontational context. That is, rather than simply expressing disagreement over the manner of managing the scandals, it was advisable to make suggestions, ask questions and request further explanation of a point of dissention. I believed that a critical issue was trust, and it had been violated. If it had been proven that an individual who was a part of the ministry, did not attempt to undermine it in any way, then that individual would be more readily heard. If it had been proven that the person's counsel and wisdom had a record of being correct and beneficial to the ministry, then the person would have a voice during those presbytery meetings. Many people sat in silence during those meetings.

Most of the younger elders grew up in that ministry and regarded Bishop Paulk as a father in the Lord. They had grown to trust his leadership and would never consider doing anything that would contradict or embarrass him, in any way. It became obvious, to me, that there were a variety of reasons that governed the degree of interaction in those presbytery meetings. First of all, the freedom of expressions in our presbytery meetings was very different in the early days when compared to the latter ones. I firmly believe that the scandals, accusations, and alleged betrayals by those who exposed or leaked confidential information about the ministry created a distrust, suspicion, and an intolerance of anything or anyone who remotely looked like an Absalom or a Judas.

In the beginning of my tenure with the ministry, the presbytery meetings were times of joy, liberty, honesty and vulnerability. There were times when the Bishop's position on a matter was challenged, but it was done in a non-confrontational manner. However, time and human misbehavior had diminished the trust level, and now there was very little honesty in our meetings.

It was during those times that I discovered the strengths and weaknesses of leaders. Their strength resided in their willingness to obey God at any cost. On the other hand, their weakness rested in their unwillingness to hear criticism or correction from others because of their wounds or hurts. Faith and stubbornness are not always distinguishable. That is, boldness and determination can be the product of both faith and stubbornness. A safeguard against such misconception is a multitude of counsel. A senior leader should surround him or herself with people who are encouraged to be honest. If such a leader believes that oneness is sameness, then he or she will be intolerant of any opinions contrary to the status quo. Disagreement is as beneficial as agreement.

It became clear, to me, that a misconception of faith and law could precipitate problems in judgments and behavior. Furthermore, this misconception was not restricted to the Cathedral. The dimension of such doctrinal confusion was confirmed during one of our church conferences when a visiting pastor came to me for counsel regarding his marriage relationship. He asked me if it were possible to have a "spiritual wife" in addition to his wife. He made reference to 1 Corinthian 9:1-5 in which Paul addressed his detractors:

> *Am I not an apostle? Am I not free? Have I not seen*
> *Jesus Christ our Lord? Are not ye my work in the*
> *Lord? If I be not an apostle unto others, yet, doubtless*
> *I am to you; for the seal of mine apostleship are ye in*

the Lord. Mine answer to them that do examine me
in this, have we not power to eat and to drink? Have
we not power to lead about a sister, a wife, as well as
other apostles, and as the brethren of the Lord, and
Cephas?

The young man felt that the reference to a "sister" gave license to the concept of "spiritual wife." A "spiritual wife," in his understanding, was a very special woman who would meet the needs that his own wife was not fulfilling. The only exception was sexual intimacy. I explained to him that the scriptural reference had no connection to such a concept and that marriage provided absolute boundaries regarding the condition and behavior of the husband and wife. Furthermore, I indicated to him that to suggest that this passage gave license to pursue a social relationship outside the boundaries of marriage for the purpose of fulfilling emotional or spiritual needs not being addressed in the marriage was not justified by faith nor any "situation ethics."

These were critical discoveries, to me, since I was looking for the causes of these consistent mistakes in judgment and behavior. I began to realize that spiritual entities masquerade themselves in natural ways. That is, what we believe spiritually will be expressed naturally.

Since the scandal involved the abuse of women, I felt that misconceptions of the Biblical norm of the male and female relationship could put individuals and entire communities at risk. While the Bible sets forth men and women as created in the image of God and being co-equal (Gen. 1-3), misinterpretation of Scriptural passages have been used to reinforce destructive behavior and justify abuse against women (1 Cor. 11,14; 1 Tim.2; Col. 3; Eph. 5; 1 Pet. 3). Many of the traditional concepts of male dominance, female submission and inferiority contribute to the reasons behind the abuse of women in the home, marketplace, and the church. There is no suggestion or proof that any of these beliefs alone cause the abuse and exploitation of women. However, these beliefs can interact with other factors and create an atmosphere where abuse may occur. The implication of a Biblical view that men should dominate women has been the justification for men to enforce control, and such misconceptions have contributed to sexual misconduct.

Sandra and I organized a conference around a book we were writing on creational order. It was a two-day meeting at a location off the campus of the Cathedral, and it was well attended by members and non-members of the church. The reports of our teaching reached the senior leadership; therefore, on Sunday morning, there were very strong statement made against our meeting and the content. There were also accusations of creating division in the ministry and organizing programs without the authority of the church. Well, Sandra and I were elders of the church and had been given liberty to pursue the writings of our books and any teaching programs that we deemed necessary. Trust and confidence had been placed in my prophetic words and counsel, and I had stood with the leadership during some of its most critical periods, so it was disappointing when I discovered that accusations were being made against our integrity. However, this taught me that the content of our teaching was touching some very critical beliefs regarding women. For example, we challenged the following misconceptions of male dominance that was embraced because of misinterpretation of the Scriptures:

1. Creation establishes God-ordained hierarchy that places the man above the woman in authority in the marriage and in the family. The husband is the head, leader, and the authority over the wife and children. The final authority in all matters always belongs to the husband or man.

2. Marriage offers specific roles for the husband and the wife. The husband is the leader who is responsible for the spiritual welfare of the family, and the wife is the submissive member.

3. The husband and wife may discuss major decisions, but the final power of the decision rests with the husband.

4. The role of providing for the family rests with the husband while the internal affairs of the home, such as raising the children, belongs to the wife.

At our conference, we taught that the male-female submission issues in biblical misinterpretation relates primarily to four topics and texts:

1. The meaning of the term kephale or head (1 Cor. 11:2-16 and Eph. 5:21-33)
2. The meaning of authentin or "authority over"

(1 Tim. 2:8-15)

3.   The creation order relationship of the male and female taken from Genesis 1-3

4.   The meaning of "submission and silence" (1 Cor. 14:34-35)

We also taught that the chronology of Eve's creation and how her role in the fall has been used erroneously as the foundation for the belief that women are morally inferior to men and should not trust their own judgment. Such traditional beliefs favor the view that women are led into spiritual error, and for that reason, it is alleged, that women should not usurp authority over the men.

Religious beliefs, due to misinterpretation of scripture that women are morally defective, unable to trust their inner sense of what is right and wrong, and that men reflect more of the divine image than women, will render women submissive to abuse and unable to confront it. When women are taught not to trust themselves, then they relinquish their power and lose their ability to confront and resist destructive behavior directed toward them.

When women are put in positions of subjection because of religious traditions, they develop characteristics such as passivity, dependence, lack of initiative, docility and the unwillingness to think and act for themselves. In fact, a male dominated religious society defines a spiritually mature woman as being submissive in the home, market place and the church, gentle, dependent, passive and finding identity through the man.

Women who submit to such a male-dominated religious

culture will have a lower self-esteem than women in a culture of equal male and female partnership. In fact, such women will assume responsibility for their abuse.

In retrospect, I now understand the reaction that Sunday morning to our teachings. What we had taught hit at the heart of a fundamental misconception of the leaders regarding women, which was probably the root source of the sinful behavior.

I have discovered that gospel, faith and behavior are inseparable entities. The quality of the gospel determines the character of faith whether it is presumption, feigned, or true (1 Tim. 1:5; 2 Tim. 1:5). Faith comes by hearing the gospel (Rom. 10:17). An internal conviction produced by hearing and believing by faith contributes to constructive or destructive behavior. As previously stated, when it is believed that faith makes one exempt from law, then there are tremendous consequences, and when the scriptures are used to create traditions that justify female submission and male dominance, the ingredients for manipulation and destructive behavior will be present.

Another critical area of belief that contributed to the crisis at the Cathedral centered around the idea of spiritual authority. Our senior leadership and others would often refer to this concept. This is a coined phrase that was popularized by Watchman Nee in his book, *Spiritual Authority*. However, the idea of authority has its origin in Scripture and first appeared in the creation narrative (Gen. 1-3; Rom. 13:1; Eph. 1:19-23; 1 Cor. 15:24). The man and woman, both made in the image of God, are endowed with specific capacities such as rationality, creativity, community, righteousness, and dominion. With these capacities, together, they are commissioned by the Lord to export the knowledge, wisdom and government of God throughout the earth. They were not commissioned to rule over or dominate one another. They were created to be co-equal, co-essential, and co-substantial. That is, creation made a distinction between male and female, but there is no idea of superiority, inferiority, nor dominance.

In the New Testament, the concept of authority is properly and completely presented and demonstrated by the Lord Jesus. A classic scripture is found in Luke 4:18:

> *The Spirit of the Lord is upon me, because he hath*
> *anointed me to preach the gospel to the poor; he*
> *hath sent me to heal the brokenhearted, to preach*
> *deliverance to the captives, and recovering of sight to*
> *the blind, and to set at liberty them that are bruised, to*
> *preach the acceptable year of the Lord.*

The Lord Jesus declared that all rule, ability, power, dominance, right, privilege, pre-eminence, superiority, jurisdiction, dominion, liberty and strength had been given to him (Matt. 9:6; 16:15-19; 21:23; 28:18; Luke 1:52; 9:1; 10:19; John 17:2; 20:19-24; Mark 13:34). This authority to rule, govern, and establish Divine government and order in the earth was delegated to the apostles (Mark 16:15-18; Matt. 28:18-20). Such authority is inseparable from the concept of the Kingdom of God and the Church (Matt. 16:19; 24:14; Luke 9:2). The agent of this authority is the Scripture and the Holy Spirit (Rom. 14:17; Mark 12:24). The Scripture is the intelligence of this authority, and the Holy Spirit is its power.

Revelation is the distinguishing factor of such authority. Furthermore, revelation is the transmission of Divine wisdom, knowledge and understanding to an individual or group; and it is also the validation of the presence of true authority (2 Cor. 10:8-18; Eph. 3:1-5; 13:1-10). While every believer has Biblical revelation, there is selective revelation in the sense that the Holy Spirit dispenses understanding and power to different individuals based upon their callings and functions. That is, there is a distinction between the leaders and congregations. There are apostles, prophets, evangelists, pastors, teachers, ministries of helps, administration and other gifts and functions that are endowed with authority based upon their callings (Rom. 12:1-8; 1 Cor. 12:1-25; Eph. 4:1-11). In essence, there are distinctions in authority based upon Divine purposes (Eph. 3:1-5). These distinctions are not based upon gender or socioeconomic status (Gal. 3:28; 5:6; 6:15; Col. 3:11).

As previously stated, I have felt that the battleground of the universal Church has always been doctrinal. It has resided in the interpretation or misinterpretation of historic truths and practices. Oftentimes, the abuse of Biblically based principles and practices has precipitated a skepticism and disdain for such truths. Again, the correction of abuse is not disuse; rather, it is proper use (1 Thess. 5:19-21; 1 Cor. 14:1-33). That is, there should be no discontinuation of Biblical truths and practices simply because they have been distorted. The correct response to such distortion should be reformation by proper application.

Regarding the crisis at the Cathedral, I felt that the personalization and misapplication of authority created a huge problem. Indeed, authority means to "rule over" and to shepherd (Acts 20:28-30; Heb. 13:7; 17: 24); however, when the misconception of male dominance and female submission is mixed with an unhealthy concept of authority, there is danger. That is, when spiritual authority generates a misconception that a person should not touch God's anointed or question leadership, then misconceptions about women will be presented as a Biblical norm. Besides, the atmosphere will create room for exploitation and abuse to occur.

It was during those times that Sandra and I wrote a book titled *Discernment*. It was in an effort to examine, among other concerns, the spirit realm of Christianity. There had been so much teaching on deliverance and demons that we wanted to know the Biblical foundation of such beliefs. Just as misinterpretation, regarding the matter of faith, gender, and authority, contributed to the crisis at the Cathedral, the spirit world was critical. Since people were being accused of being under the influence of spirits, whenever they questioned or resisted authority, it became apparent that this was a critical source of the problem.

Spirits may refer to a wide range of the human, the demonic, and the angelic (Gen. 16:9; 19:1, 31:11; Josh. 5:13-15; Judg. 6:22; 1 Sam. 17:23, 28:7-19; Dan. 10:5-21; Acts 8:5-7, 20-24; 12:7-10, 21-23; 13:6-11, 16-19). Human beings can be a "house of spirits" (1 Cor. 14:32; 17:16; 2 Cor. 2:11). Demons are unclean, evil and destructive forces (Mark 1:23-25; 9:25; Acts 16:16-18). Angels are "ministering spirits" (Heb. 1:14; Acts 27:23-24). Discernment is the ability to distinguish between a whole range of spirits that may be operating in a given space and time (1 Cor. 12:10). This illumination or distinguishing is only possible by the Holy Spirit operating through the spirit of the redeemed believer. This discernment is principle-based and is conditioned by knowledge and understanding of the Scripture and personal opinions, conceptions, and experiences (1 Kings 3:9; Matt. 16:3; Heb. 5:14).

It is possible to have misconception regarding the presence of spirits and their operation based upon religious conditioning. For example, it is possible to negate the existence of the spirit world and believe that all human sicknesses, diseases, and misbehaviors can be explained and treated by science and medicine. On the contrary, it is possible to attribute all human dysfunctions to the spirit world and depend upon deliverance as the only correction. One extreme denies the existence of the spirit realm and seeks to treat depression, anxiety, addiction, and immorality, using scientific counsel, medication, and self-discipline. The other extreme relegates all such dysfunctions to the presence and operation of spiritual forces and believes that deliverance can only be achieved through the binding of spirits, long hours praying and fasting, and the verbal denunciation of curses of all kinds. Of course, a healthy approach would be the integration of appropriate principles and practices from both extremes. Therefore, discernment would be necessary to determine the problem, cause, and treatment.

As indicated earlier, the crisis at the Cathedral was a result of a number of factors. For one, religious traditions that were the products of misconception and misapplication of historic principles and practices were introduced, and this was true of spirits and discernment. Even though the approach at the Cathedral was well balanced with the integration of faith and science, there were some questionable practices. This was especially true regarding the labeling of certain individuals who disagreed with certain aspects of the ministry. Rather than specifically accusing people in strategic teachings, during the corporate worship services or at other gatherings, would include references to spirits of control, disobedience, rebellion, anger, resentment, rejection, competition, bitterness, and a host of other factors that were supposed to possess or influence people who disagreed with principles and practices being presented by the church. Since no believer would embrace the idea of being controlled, in any manner, by an evil spirit, such suggestions became powerful tools of manipulation and control. For example, I was indirectly accused of having a spirit of control because I objected to the newly adopted advertisement practices. We had historically criticized other ministries for using public billboards, and now, we were adopting the same practices. I was, no doubt, offended by such a strategy to silence my voice. As a result, I did not relent, and I persisted in my position, for it was hypocritical to practice what we condemned. This revealed, to me, the subtle control and manipulation that was prevalent during the days of the scandal.

Nevertheless, the existence of the spirit realm, free will and self-discipline, should not be denied. Both are important. However, during the latter phases of the life of the ministry when questionable theological and doctrinal material were introduced by a few of the resident leaders and visiting speakers, there were reactions and responses from the people. The public endorsement of homosexuality, universalism, and the denial of the deity of Jesus and inspiration of the Scripture precipitated reactions and responses from the congregation. The Biblical foundations of the congregation had been challenged, assaulted, and even denied.

It can be seen that religious traditions, such as beliefs

and convictions, masqueraded themselves in attitudes and behavioral patterns. In addition, misconceptions, whether intentional or unintentional, regarding faith, spiritual authority, gender, and the spirit realm, have tremendous consequences.

The construction of the Cathedral

Ordination to bishop with Earl Paulk and my wife, Sandra, in 1999

Earl Paulk and Clariece Paulk

Annual Harvest Run, June 1981, Atlanta, with Earl and Norma Paulk

Early days preaching at Chapel Hill Harvester Church

Our first visit to South Africa in 1987

Preaching at first inter-racial conference in South Africa in 1987

Mission trip to El Salvador

Conference 1993:
Bishop Willie Chambliss,
Rev. Eddie Traut, Donna
Summer

Conference 1997:
Pastor Collette L. Gunby,
Pastor Euthemnia Avery Jr,
Pastor Wiley Jackson Jr,
Elder Marvin Sapp,
Rev. Dale C. Bronner

Conference 2001:
Dr. Mike Murdock,
Anthony Hudgins,
Bishop Fred Addo,
Bishop Charles Agyin
Asare, Bishop Matthew
Addae-Mensah,
Bishop Joel & Pastor
Yonette Thomas

Conference 2001:
Dr. Bill Hamon, Ed Silvoso,
Dick Mills, Tony Perkins,
Jim Hodges, Jane Hansen,
Dr. Sharon Stone

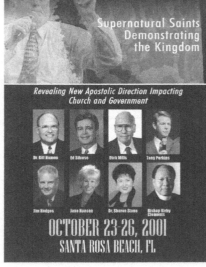

CHAPTER 11

GIFTS, CALLINGS AND SANCTIFICATION

A s previously mentioned, we were often questioned about the nature of the scandals during our travels. One of the consistent questions related to the concept of anointing. Since anointing was the presence of the Holy Spirit, how could the Spirit not be grieved over these matters? How could such immoral and unethical activities be prevalent in individuals with the appearance of an anointing? Are the gifts and callings of God without repentance (Rom. 11:29)? Can individual ministries never be in jeopardy regardless of the character flaws and misbehavior of the individuals (Matt. 7:21; 21:43; Heb. 6:4-6)? Are leaders held accountable to a different set of standards from others (Acts 20:25-38; Heb. 13:17)? These issues were of major concern and people desired to know. In fact, many sincerely felt that our anointing was being compromised because we maintained our association with the ministry. Sandra and I searched the Scriptures for answers.

First of all, Christianity is a propositional faith with specific beliefs and standards to be embraced and acted upon (Acts 4:12; Rom. 10:8-15; 2 Tim. 3:16; Heb. 11:6; Eph. 4:4-6). Some of these fundamental propositions include the deity of Jesus Christ; the virgin birth; the inspiration of Scripture;

necessity of spiritual regeneration; reality of sin; privilege of prayer; and the responsibility for evangelism. Faith represents our contractual relationship with God and it is initiated from hearing and believing Divine information . As stated earlier, the character of faith is directly dependent upon the integrity of the information. For example, if the information presented is not complete or deficient in content, then it is possible for the individuals to believe the wrong things and accept privileges that are not truly available (2 Tim. 2:16-19; Col. 1-2; Gal. 1:6-12; 3:1). This, we found to be true when individuals came to us for counsel and claimed to have been given authorization for their sexual misbehavior. This was feigned faith and rebellion with knowledge, for they were not without an understanding of Biblical standards of sexual conduct. Finally, Christianity is universal in its application without respect of race, gender, age, or socioeconomic status (Rev. 5:9; 14:6; Rom. 10:13). Faith produces believers who may have different gifts, callings and responsibilities. But the command to present our bodies as living sacrifice holy and acceptable unto God applies to all without distinction (Rom. 12:1,2). This is the norm of Christianity.

The gifts and callings are conditional graces bestowed upon individuals (1 Cor. 12; Eph. 4:11). The atmosphere of the operation of these graces is holiness, which is the emulation of Christ Jesus. It is not simply external displays in clothing, food preferences, and speech preferences. That is, holiness is an internal regeneration and transformation of heart that is expressed in character and integrity (Rom. 2:28-29; 12:1-2; Heb.13:21). Paul exhorts Timothy to be an example of the believer in character, faith, and behavior (1 Tim. 4:12).

It is proposed that the operation of gifts and callings can

be compromised and put in jeopardy when there is a lack of integrity. Such misbehavior is referred to as sin. For the sake of clarity, let us examine the concept of sin. There are two words that describe this state of estrangement from God:

> Hamartia which is missing the mark is a principle or source of action, or an inward element producing acts (Rom. 3:9, 5:12,13, 20; 6:1,2; 7:7). It is also viewed as a governing principle or power (Rom. 6:6)…an organized power, acting through the members of the body, though the seat of sin is in the will (the body is the organizing instrument). It is also used in a generic way as inclusive of wrong doing and lawlessness.

> Hamartema, on the other hand, is an act of disobedience to divine law. Notice John 1:29: "Behold the Lamb of God, who taketh away the sin (not sins) of the world." This means a condition of sin or a course of sin. Hence, Christ's death takes away, not the tendency to miss the mark or to act unrighteous, but the estrangement or the offense between God and humankind is removed.

The above information is simply to set forth the idea of sin, its remission and the admonition to discontinue its practice. It helps us understand an obvious presence of grace among us. I also opened my mind to the reality that grace and mercy were not the toleration of any form of human misbehavior.

In our contemporary religious culture, sin is occasionally restricted to sex and money. As previously mentioned, sin is not only missing the mark, it is also a state of existence contrary to Divine standards, parameters, intentions, and purpose. It is humanity acting in a manner contrary to being a human. Hence, sin is a generic term that covers a variety of intentional and unintentional transgressions, mistakes, and activities. Above all, it is a breach of the Divine/human relationship.

James uses the word "conceived," which indicates an incubation period in which ideas, perceptions, values, and objectives are mentally considered and rationalized in the mind until such thoughts precipitate behavior (Jam. 1:13-15). As such, the idea of missing the mark can be intentional or unintentional. Even though standards are the expression of the ideal of God for human behavior, there are those who are deceived or seduced to misbehave, and there are those who breach the standards with full knowledge of their behavior. Peter speaks of those who are "willingly ignorant" and "wrestle the Scripture to their own destruction" (2 Pet. 3:16). Hence, there is misbehavior with knowledge (rebellion) and misbehavior without knowledge (gullibility, ignorance, or immaturity). The Lord Jesus disclosed this distinction between rebellion and ignorance when he asked the Jews if they understood His teachings (Matt. 22:29). If they had not understood and disobeyed, then their sins were forgiven. If they understood and still disobeyed, then their sins remained. Rebellion is disobedience with knowledge.

In addition, there is the issue of the frequency and implication of a violation of Divine standards. Is the transgression a first-time offense or a repeated one? Does the mistake only involve the individual, or does it directly affect others? Are there precipitating factors that contribute to the mistakes of the individual such as faulty counsel, misleading instructions, and even deception? For example, there was a young man sent by

God with specific instructions for the discharge of his ministry (1 Kings 13). After the young messenger dispensed his duties and even resisted the temptation and threat of the king, he was later convinced to disobey by an unidentified old prophet and suffered the consequences of his disobedience (1 Kings 13:24). This young prophet disobeyed a mandate of the Lord with full knowledge of the mandate. He had respect to the person and office of the old prophet. This is called rebellion or disobedience with knowledge. To the contrary, Paul admits that his persecution of the Church was done in ignorance and unbelief (Tim. 1:12-13). Again, Peter speaks of those who are "willingly ignorant" and wrestle with the Scriptures for their own destruction (2 Pet. 3:5, 16).

What is the significance of this discussion? Our original consideration relates to gifts, callings and sanctification. A critical concern is whether there can be an "anointing" or "gifting" or "calling" in an individual who continuously transgresses the standards of moral and ethical righteousness (1 Cor. 6:9-11; Eph. 5:5). We have said gifts and callings are set aside with specific functions and standards of performance. That is, individuals so enabled by the Spirit as leaders or saints are to conduct themselves as an example for others to follow (1 Tim. 4:12; 2 Thes. 3:7,9). This sanctification motif sets forth the fact that continuous unethical and immoral behavior is intolerable for a leader or a believer. However, gifts and callings are not always sanctified. Even in our contemporary faith communities, there have been public ministers who have continuously violated the principle of sanctification. However, the continuous violation of Biblical norms of sanctification eventually compromised the gift and calling.

The critical question is whether an individual can continue in such misbehavior without consequences. The principle of sowing and reaping sets forth the reality that all misbehavior has consequences (Gal. 6:7-8). Even though the fruits of such misbehavior may not be readily revealed, the continuation of such behavior should not be misinterpreted as Divine approval or tolerance. Ecclesiastes 8:11 reveals the misconception regarding the delayed judgment of evil. Because judgment against an evil work is not executed immediately then those involved tend to conclude that the lack of Divine judgment is an indication of mercy, toleration, or accommodation. This concept of lawlessness is often supported by a misinterpretation of Paul when he writes that "all things are lawful but all things are not expedient"(1 Cor. 6:12; 10:23). This reference by Paul is not associated with the permission for unethical behavior.

Gifts and callings are to be executed in an atmosphere of holiness, and there are absolutely no exceptions to such standards. Deviation from such standards of operation ultimately ends in failure.

CHAPTER 12

RACE, CULTURE AND TOLERANCE

We are citizens of the 60s, but we escaped most of the perils and experienced a lot of historical moments. For example, I witnessed the desegregation of the University of Georgia by two of my high school classmates, Hamilton Holmes and Charlene Hunter in 1961. That same year, I was chosen with five others to desegregate Georgia Institute of Technology. My parent dismissed the idea and off to Morehouse I went. Morehouse was a better school for me with its rich heritage and the presence of Dr. Benjamin Mays, a pioneer in life. The Civil Rights Movement was in its prime, and Atlanta was on the agenda. During one of my classes in the gymnasium, a man slowly walked into the room and sat directly next to me. As his identity became known, the entire class stood and applauded him. It was none other than Dr. Martin Luther King, Jr. Once he was introduced, he graciously moved to the front of the class and began to outline his strategy to desegregate the lunch counters in Atlanta. It was an exciting moment for all of us in attendance, especially for me. That morning launched the involvement of a zealous group of college students in the historic Civil Rights Movement.

After Morehouse and a brief stint in the working world, I

went off to Howard University School of Dentistry for a most successful four years. I remember the motivation speech given to me by a local physician in Atlanta before my departure. He said, "Clements, in four years, you will be four years older with a degree, or you will be four years older without a degree. Either way, you will be four years older." I chose the age and degree combination. After Howard University, I was encouraged to pursue a graduate program in dentistry at Boston University School of Graduate Dentistry with a full stipend.

Boston was experiencing a sociopolitical crisis because of the desegregation of its school system. It reminded us of the 1960s in the South with its share of violence except the protest was being initiated and sustained by the non-Black populations. Interestingly, enough, I would be the first Afro-American to enter the graduate program in prosthetic dentistry at Boston. Moreover, my family would be the first to unknowingly attempt to violate a lease law in Massachusetts when we sought to rent a house in a certain area of Boston. We were unaware that the community had a law that forbade cattle, sheep, goats and Negroes from living within its borders. When the neighbors threatened the owner of the house with violence, he refused to rent us the house. The matter reached the ears of a class-action lawyer who filed a lawsuit on our behalf. The lawsuit overturned the lease law. We eventually purchased a house in Duxbury, Massachusetts.

We thoroughly enjoyed our two years in Boston, and we were introduced to many people, cultures and ethnic groups. My department chairman at the university was Italian, and he was very familiar with the sociopolitical climate of Boston during those days. Since I was the first Black student in that department, he made sure that I was treated fairly. In fact, at the beginning of the program, no patients were being assigned to me for treatment even though all of my classmates had a whole lot of patients. He knew why and immediately corrected that issue. I remember that one of my first patients was a member of the Mafia. I will always remember the words of my mentor when he said, "KC, if you have ever done painless dentistry, then now is the time." Although we all were very nervous, we laughed, and I did painless dentistry that day!

The experiences in Boston broadened our awareness of different people since my classmates were from North and South America, Europe, South Africa, and Asia. We occasionally interacted on a personal level and discovered that we all had lived within the confines of our nationalities, cultures and ethnic groups. Those social gatherings and our personal interactions often shattered some our negative stereotypes of one another. Also it became very obvious, to me, that the correction of prejudice was knowledge and experience. Long-standing misconceptions about other racial groups can rapidly be discredited during moments of vulnerability and honesty.

Boston came to an end, but not before we experienced an interesting phenomena one night. Sandra and I were sound asleep, and both of us were awakened to see a large Bible encircled by a bright light. We were startled, but we were not afraid. The vision remained for a few moments, and then it vanished from our sight. Of course, we talked for hours about what we had seen, but we had no understanding of its meaning; however, the meaning was later revealed.

After submitting my thesis, we packed, and headed back to Washington DC. I had an obligation to teach at the dental school for two years as a professor of dentistry. Once we got settled at a temporary residence, we made every effort to purchase a home and start a private practice. Our efforts produced no fruit. During this time of frustrated effort, we were introduced to the world of Holy Ghost ministration. During a visit to a Women's Aglow meeting, we received a prophetic word that spoke about our future in ministry. That same night, we received another prophecy from our pastor about a call into the ministry. Needless to say, this was all very surprising to both of us, but there was no resistance to this new thought in either of us. Interestingly, enough, while the house and dental practice had failed to materialize, an amazing change in our schedule occurred. Rather than remaining at the university for two years, we felt compelled to return to Atlanta to pursue an opportunity to practice, dentistry. The university released me from the balance of my contract. In retrospect, if we had been successful in purchasing a home and starting a practice, we could not have left Washington in such a hurry. So after spending a year in Washington, we were off to Atlanta.

The South was experiencing the "browning of the churches." Churches were being integrated, and racial and cultural stereotypes were being confronted. While Chapel Hill Harvester had previously been an all-White congregation, the senior leaders understood the Pauline perspective that in Christ, there was neither Black nor White. They made every effort to dispel any signs of prejudicial thought and behavior that would have been latent or obvious among the staff and the congregation. However, there was still the belief in racial distinction regarding music, preaching styles, and social behavior. For example, when the senior leaders made plans to attract more Blacks to the church, they were convinced that inviting Black preachers and gospel singers and musicians would work magic. Since my preaching and singing style did not fit the racial stereotype, many that believed some fiery gospel preaching and singing would be the catalyst. After all, this was the strategy that the senior leader had used in one of his previous all-White churches. He invited some Black students form Atlanta University to come to the church to confront the prejudice of the all-White congregation and to create a race-friendly atmosphere. I discovered that oneness is not sameness. Additionally, I realized that an integrated church can still be a segregated church when the various cultural and ethnic groups maintain their distinctions.

Sandra and I were committed to God and had no internal racial biases. Our travels had made us "race-friendly" and culturally sensitive. This was affirmed when a member of the largest Pentecostal group in South Africa made a visit to the church. His name was Justus DuPlessi, a White Afrikaner and the brother of David DuPlessi, who was known as Mr. Pentecost because of his pioneering effort to facilitate communication between the Roman Catholics and the Pentecostals. Justus attended all of our services for the entire week, and he was even present at our presbytery meetings. Interesting, enough, he would always select a seat near or next to me. At the end of his visit, Justus revealed to Bishop Paulk that the Lord had sent him to America to find a Black man, without a chip on his shoulder, to come to South Africa and be the first non-White to speak at their churches and conferences. He said that he had traveled throughout many churches in America and had not found such a man. However, he confided in Bishop Paul that his search had ended with me, because I was the man.

In 1987, Sandra and I made our inaugural visit to South Africa during its apartheid regime. It was a country divided by race and cultures. The social groups were identified as being Black, Colored, Indian or White. The Apostolic Faith Mission was our host, and its churches were divided into the same groups. There was no interchange between the churches and each of them, although united by doctrine, worshipped in different places. I was the first Black to speak at all the different churches and at their annual Worker's Conference that was reserved for the White leaders only. I remember the night that I was introduced to the conference by Justus DuPlessi. He described the ministry of Chapel Hill Harvester as being a ministry of many different racial and cultural groups and how I was one of the chief pastors. After my message, which lasted thirty minutes because of the live translation, I gave a prophetic word that had been impressed upon my heart before I left the states. I remember it to this day because I had written it on a small piece of paper:

> *O South Africa! Though you are the scourge of nations today because of your troubles, a day will come when nations and countries will come to your shores to see what you have done by the power of God.*

I was quite nervous and uncertain of the response I would receive. There was a brief pause as I closed my Bible and turned to take my seat, and then a tumultuous sound came from that massive congregation of White Afrikaners as they stood and began to cheer, applaud and worship the Lord. Many began to literally run around the aisles, and some even fell upon their faces.

After the service and all of the handshaking and hugs had ceased, a host of newspaper reporters converged upon us and began to ask, "Who are you, and by what authority do you say these things?" Some thought that I was an ambassador from America. I simply said that I was a preacher.

That prophecy opened the door for us throughout South Africa, for it had come from a Black man! In fact, one of my messages reached the ears of President Botha, who was the Prime Minister at the time. In the message, I said that He had been trained by God and was chosen to deliver South Africa. He responded that what I had said about him was true. He had been trained as a theologian who pursued politics. He had a heart for God, but he was not able to bring deliverance for fear of the consequences.

While the prophecy opened some doors, it seemed to close others and precipitate suspicion among the Blacks, Colored and Indian factions of the churches. Because I had been invited by Justus DuPlessi, who was White Afrikaner, many of the non-White members believed I was simply a hired voice for the White apartheid regime. That experience taught me the significance of trust and how it could be established.

It was during our second visit in 1988, that I spoke at the first inter-racial conference in Durban, where all of the groups attended. It was a very tense meeting, and although the dissension between the factions was not obvious, it was rather present. The facial expression and the body language of many present was a message in itself. The distrust was present until I gave prophetic words to four men sitting in the congregation. I had no knowledge of either of them except their social identity. After the meeting, one of the Colored leaders revealed to me that each of the men was the head of the four groups of Blacks, Colored, Indian and White factions of the church. However, the word given to the White leader, who was also the head of the entire Apostolic Faith Mission organization, was very specific in identifying the major crisis facing the organization, so the non-White factions accepted my ministry. In fact, many of the Black, Colored, and Indian leaders secretly came to us and revealed how their suspicions and doubts had been erased that night because of the prophecy. That taught me that one word from God settles all controversy.

Sandra and I returned to the states after one month of ministry in South Africa. We were, no doubt, excited and anxious to give reports to the church. The opportunity was given to me to preach and give a testimony of the South Africa visit. The people were so gracious and expressed their thanksgiving to the Lord with applause and shouts of praise. Nevertheless, there was a small minority of leaders who slandered my report and claimed that the success of the campaign was only due to our association with Chapel Hill Harvester Church. It was as if nothing or no one had value outside of their association with the local ministry. I was stunned and greatly disappointed, but this slander revealed some characteristics that are often evident among strong and dominant leaders. It was recorded that when David entered the city after one of his triumphant victories, that the people cried out, "Saul has slain a thousand, but David has slain ten thousand" (1 Sam. 18:7-9). Such a response from the people provoked Saul to feel obsolete and insignificant. In fact, from that time, Saul sought to kill David. While there is no obvious parallel between that historic encounter and what happened that Sunday morning, it taught me an invaluable lesson. Strong leaders must lead without any distractions. People can create competition and unnecessary comparison among leaders by their expressions of appreciation. Furthermore, insecurities and feelings of being obsolete can influence the minds of the most effective leaders. My role as a leader must be to assist the leader without distraction. I would make every effort to diffuse any forms of competition or comparison that arose from among the people.

Nevertheless, all of these events seemed to come to a focus during the later phases of the scandal at the Cathedral. It must be remembered that the congregation of the Cathedral was once multi-cultural, multi-racial, multi-national, and multi-generational. There were members from Africa, Asia, Europe, South America, North America, Australia, and the Caribbean. The senior leadership of the Cathedral had been very pro-active in the racial desegregation activities of the 60s and had intentionally transformed the racial composition of the congregation. Toward the apex of the scandal, however, many members departed. It was claimed, by the senior leaders, that the departure of the White members was an expression of prejudice. Nevertheless, the reasons for the departure of members and leaders from the Cathedral were just as complex as the reasons that brought them to the ministry in the first place. For example, many came because of the preaching, music, social programs, proximity of the church to their residences, and the social acceptability of inter-racial marriages. The factors that attracted them and kept them were also relational, for they had formed friendships during their membership. Nevertheless, toward the latter phases of the scandal, the majority of the congregation was Black. It was alleged that Black members were more forgiving and tolerant of moral and ethical misbehavior among their leaders. This surfaced some very old misconceptions and prejudices that Whites were more moral and ethical than Blacks.

As it became obvious that there would be no revival of the ministry, there was a transfer of the leadership to the son of one of the founders. I was asked by one of the senior leaders to give my perspective of the ministry and some of the racial overtones that were circulating within and outside the church. I quoted Dr. King: "Unjust suffering is redemptive." This set forth the proposition that persecution and discrimination creates patience, endurance and strength. Sociopolitical oppression makes people weaker or stronger. If there had been a reason for the once multi-racial congregation becoming all-Black, the reason did not reside in some alleged tolerance of immorality or unethical behavior. Compassion, forgiveness, and tolerance were not racial nor cultural specific. There was a principle to be realized. If anyone allowed the mistakes and failures of a few to control and dictate his or her life and even cause him or her to abandon his or her faith, that is definitely a sign of idolatry. Most of the churches in America were polarized around race, culture, or ethnic values. Chapel Hill Harvester/Cathedral was no different. Our misconception was simply that we assumed that the presence and work of the Holy Spirit among us during all of those previous years was an indication that the latent prejudices and racial stereotypes were no longer among us. We were still carnal, and the fruits were simply being expressed. However, I commended all who remained with the ministry, for it was a testimony of maturity and not racial pride.

CHAPTER 13

THE WAY OF THE LORD

As Sandra and I traveled among the network churches and conferences, we were frequently questioned about the scandals at the Cathedral. Our family and friends desired information, also. Some of the questions were: Did you know about this scandal before it was made public? The answer to that question was not simple since there had been previous rumors or allegations. As an elder, what did you think when you first heard about it? Why are you staying at the church? We were disappointed that our personal integrity was questioned. When we became aware of the allegations, we were shocked. We felt betrayed since those who were accused had professed their innocence for years. We went to the Lord in prayer for guidance and comfort. This was a terrible thing, and it involved people whom we knew and trusted. Because all the individuals involved were in leadership and a part of the staff, factions were being formed between those who believed the allegations and those who refused to believe them. Because the accused and the accusers confided in me, I often found myself serving as a peacemaker between individuals who did not desire peace but clamored for vengeance, judgment or exoneration of any guilt. In fact, I was once accused of walking with the enemy simply because I reached out to some of the individuals who left the church. The senior leaders claimed that anyone who fellowshipped with people who had left the church were the enemies of God. Because Sandra and I remained at the church, we were accused of being a part of the scandal and supported the people who were accused. Those were very challenging times to our souls and the constant bombardment of questions and even allegations were a source of great disappointment. Nevertheless, Sandra and I resolved to seek the Lord for wisdom and counsel and to remain at our place of ministry.

By this time, the tremendous accomplishments of this ministry were almost eclipsed by the knowledge of the scandals. It saddened Sandra and I to listen to the media commentaries about the scandals, surrounding Archbishop Paulk, for they would magnify the scandal but failed to make any reference to the many accomplishments. The dwindling congregation and the absence of familiar faces among us also made us sad. Nevertheless, the worship of God in preaching, teaching, praying, thanksgiving, singing, dancing and various expressions of the arts did not diminish in faith nor in excellence.

I must admit that throughout the progression of the scandals, the thing that commanded my attention was the way of the Lord. I desired to understand what the Lord already knew. In my heart, I felt that this entire experience was not simply about human mistakes and failures. Quite to the contrary, this was a God story and a tremendous revelation of the mercy, grace and love of the Lord was being demonstrated. During a time of prayer and meditation, I was impressed with Psalm 9:16, which states that the Lord is known by the judgments that He executes. That is, to understand His way is to observe His choices and decisions. It was important, to me, to witness what the Lord did and what He did not do. He obviously sees what we cannot see. This was a source of comfort and assurance to me, for I needed to understand the hope that was within me for this ministry. I began to look beyond the obvious human drama and desperately seek to understand how and why the ministry had been sustained for years despite all the issues at hand.

I discovered that prayer reveals our concepts of God. I listened to the public prayers of people and observed their requests, which expressed their fundamental understanding of the nature and character of God. In fact, during my early years in ministry, I would pray long and loud. I was convinced that it was necessary to give the Lord privileged information, so I spent extensive time trying to inform heaven. In retrospect, I can now imagine what was going on in heaven during my "warfare vigilance." I can imagine the angels asking questions: "What is he asking and why is it taking him so long to say it? Can't he do that for himself? What is the meaning behind all the shouting, waving of the hands and shaking of the head?" I am certain that such a heavenly dialogue did not occur, but my prayers expressed my belief that God would do nothing until I shook heaven. Gradually, though, I began to understand Divine liability and human responsibility. In essence, there were some things that God would not do. The management of the affairs at the Cathedral was in our hands. If we knew His will, which was repentance, faith, forgiveness, restoration and recovery, then human effort could be effective. Our battle was not with the devil or flesh and blood, but with the Lord. We were unwilling to submit to His will.

Well, I discovered that there are two prayers that God will

not answer. First, He will not respond to a request for Him to do again what He has already done. Second, He will not do what He has enabled us to do. For example, during many of my visits to other churches, the leaders would gather around me before the service and pray fervently that I would receive a double anointing and that every word that I preached would only be the words of the Lord. Well, that was a tall order. God was being asked to set aside my humanity and make me a robot so that my message would simply be a recording from heaven. Furthermore, the anointing that I have was deemed insufficient for them, so they were praying for a more powerful one. While I offered no resistance to those fervent prayers, I felt that they would not be answered. I knew that my message would be a mixture of the Divine and the human. Furthermore, the presence of the Holy Spirit in me was the anointing.

As previously stated, God was the source of our conflict and not the devil. When we submit to God in thought, attitude, and behavior, then we are resisting the devil and he will flee. The fundamental problem resides either in ignorance of Divine ways or simply a refusal to comply with Divine values, objectives, and strategies. For example, I was often called upon to resolve conflicts in ministries and offer some viable solutions to some very difficult problems. In some instances, my response could trigger an avalanche of reactions. I found solace in the narrative between the Lord and Jeremiah when the prophet complained of his inabilities (Jer. 1). The response of the Spirit to the prophet served as a fundamental recipe for obedience. The Spirit simply told Jeremiah that he was to do what was revealed, say what he heard, go where he was sent, and remain or leave when he was instructed. To this day, I refer to this as the Jeremiah Principle.

It serves as a source confidence in all my matters even until this day.

During the crisis at the Cathedral, there were so many different opinions and strategies offered for the resolution of the conflicts. While the numerous accusations of immorality and unethical conduct were not yet proven, there was a media frenzy that precipitated a public opinion poll. Some of these opinions recommended the expulsion of the key leadership and the installation of a transitional leadership team. There were demands for a public confession of guilt and apology. Some accusations were centered around an alleged deficiency of the local presbytery of elders. The accusers stated that we should have been more confrontational, and we should have demanded repentance. Other opinions recommended the desertion of the entire congregation, the shutting down of all Cathedral operations, and the selling of the property. There were even outcries for a legal response and the prosecution of the alleged offenders.

During one of my visits to an international gathering of pastors and leaders, an inquiry was made about a moral and ethical crisis surrounding a highly public and creditable leader. The phrase, "due process," was introduced as a critical factor in the resolution of the scandal. As I listened to the very lively discussion among some of the most experienced pastors and leaders, I was saddened by the harshness of some and the legalism of others. Some simply recommended the dismissal of the accused leader along with a public reprimand from the group. Others strongly believed that all ministry assignments should be canceled for some indefinite period. During their discussion, they were all aware that I was in the midst of a similar crisis at the Cathedral, so they asked for my comment. As I stood to speak, I remember being strongly impressed with the thought that any due process should not exclude the revelation of the Holy Spirit. I suggested that while much of the discussion that I had heard revolved around various denominational backgrounds and discipline, there was a need to discover if our recommendations seemed good to us and the Holy Ghost. Needless to say, my comments precipitated a very long discussion. I began to understand that in a multitude of counsel, there can be both safety and danger.

A critical factor in the identity and management of the crisis at the Cathedral was the Biblical context in which it was placed. In essence, there were efforts to look for Biblical principles that would provide some understanding. While Old Testament examples of rebellion and failure among kings, prophets and even nations were prevalent, there were no New Testament principles. The defection of Demas (2 Tim. 4:10), the failure of John Mark (Acts 15:37-39), the denial of Peter (Matt. 26:69-75; Mark 14:66-72; Luke 22:55-62; John 18:17-27) and the persecution of the Church by Saul (Acts 8:3; 9:1-8; Gal. 1:13) were not moral or ethical issues. While there were strong public opinions that the entire church was either in a state of denial of reality or attempting to exonerate guilt, the leaders and the people sought to discover a Divine perspective.

The dealings of the Lord with those who disobeyed His commandments is a study in itself. For example, Saul is dismissed for his transgression (1 Sam. 13:1-23) while David received a strong reprimand and was allowed to remain in office (2 Sam. 12:1-24). Hezekiah was convicted and sentenced to death but received healing and additional years to live when he repented

(Isa. 37-38). Paul's own testimony was that he persecuted the church and wasted it, but he received grace from the Lord and eventually preached the very things he once sought to destroy (Gal. 1:13-17). In our contemporary society, the scandal of immorality and unethical behavior among some very public leaders and the manner of their recovery had precipitated a great degree of concern. While some had been dismissed and fallen from the public eye, there were others who only received a light reprimand for some very notorious scandals. Was there a due process of dealing with such transgression? How significant was public opinion and consensus thinking in the process? And finally, was it possible that revelation was needed for the resolution of the crisis?

In consideration of such questions, the prophet Isaiah makes a clear distinction between heavenly and earthly perceptions:

For my thoughts are not your thoughts, neither are your ways my ways, saith the Lord.
Isaiah 55:8

While there were many questions and suggested solutions and strategies, were they contrary to Divine judgment? The idea that leaders were not dismissed from their public ministry was untenable to people within and without the ministry. Those who were accused continued to declare their innocence despite strong evidence to the contrary. The individuals who brought accusations against the ministry and against the key leaders were "demonized" and accused of being the enemies of God. All of this caused many to assume that there was an absence of Divine judgment and an inappropriate function of the local elders. Despite all of the external and even internal recommendations for the resolution of the crisis, was there another way? Was the crisis actually being correctly managed?

There are numerous schools of theological thought regarding the treatment of leadership failure,. and many of these opinions were expressed during this crisis. The prophetical literature is very clear regarding the consequences when shepherds fail:

> *And the word of the Lord came unto me saying, Son of man prophesy against the shepherds of Israel, prophesy and say unto them , Thus saith the Lord God unto the shepherds; woe be to the shepherds of Israel that do feed themselves, should not the shepherd feed the flock? Therefore, O ye shepherds, hear the word of the Lord, thus saith the Lord, Behold I am against the shepherds and I will require my flock at their hand, and cause them to cease from feeding my flock; neither shall the shepherds feed themselves any more for I will deliver my flock from their mouth that they may not be meat for them.* Ezek. 34:2, 7, 8-10

Based on this scripture, there is a Divine judgment against shepherds, leaders of a flock, or congregation. However, is this verse applicable in this modern setting, and if so, how? The crisis at the Cathedral was more localized since it involved the transgression of a few individuals and was not a negligence of the congregation. The congregation was cared for by those leaders and staff assigned to that responsibility.

There was an effort to excuse the transgression of the few elders by creating a category of sin. While there are transgressions that are done willingly, unwillingly, ignorantly, and with knowledge, can there be categories of sin: Flesh sins and spirit sins? Are the mistakes mentioned by Paul that prohibits an inheritance in the Kingdom of God catalogued as sins of the flesh (Eph. 5:5) while those offences that turn away from faith in God a different set of sins without repentance (Heb. 6:6)? In essence, are there social sins and spiritual sins? Was David's transgression with Bathsheba a sin of the flesh while Saul's disobedience was a sin of the spirit? While this proposition was set forth by a few, the consequences of misbehavior were quite prevalent. Even when there is Divine forgiveness, there are still human consequences. Often, these consequences are expressed in loss of public credibility and significant diminishing of the ministry. The Scripture is true: "He that troubles his own house shall inherit the wind" (Prov. 11:29).

It is my opinion that the judgment of God was present during this crisis. The most definitive judgment of God is not simply to take a life but to let it continue. Repentance and the awakened consciousness of the cause and implications of human misbehavior cannot be accomplished in death. A dead individual cannot repent. To dismiss an accused individual from public responsibilities seems to be the highest sentence; however, it is not. To demand that an individual live and continue to function in the very environment and among the same people where an indictment has been made is itself a judgment. Indeed, there are times when the Divine judgment is to step down and step away, but that was not the sentence here. There is a greater judgment in living than in dying, and it must be noted that all misbehavior has within itself a judgment.

It is also interesting to note that the precipitating factor or moral failure of a few received a greater level of attention. Indeed, leaders should be held to a greater standard of integrity. Nevertheless, the entire redeemed community was not free of sin. Sin is not restricted to sex and money. Sin is acting in a way that is not normal for a human. In creation, humanity was not constituted to sin. Sin is a contradiction to human nature. In fact, of the seven sins that God hates, they can all be present among the congregation of the saints (Prov. 6:16-19).

> *There are six things the LORD hates, seven that are detestable to him: **haughty eyes, a lying tongue, hands that shed innocent blood, a heart that devises wicked schemes, feet that are quick to rush into evil, a false witness who pours out lies and a man who stirs up dissension among brothers***

Likewise, among the saints, there can be the presence of discord, arrogance, desertion, disbelief, and vengeance.

It is during these times that much is learned about the ways of the Lord. His ways are made known through His judgment, counsel, and choices (Psalm 9:16; 89:14; 145:17; Jer. 9:24; Rom. 3:4-6; 9:14-23). Because His ways are distinctively different and higher than the ways of His leaders and people, confusion and controversy often erupts because a matter is not managed according to popular consensus. This is the case here. Public and religious opinion and consensus thinking do not always represent Divine counsel. While the scripture says, "In a multitude of counsel there is safety," (Prov. 11:14) this is only true of the counsel that is correct and righteous, for a lot of people can also be wrong. For that reason, the consensus opinions of leaders and people and even the judgment of the public media can represent treatment of spiritual and ethical failures in a way that may be foreign to the ways of the Lord. As I mentioned before, there was an outcry from many that the alleged offenders should be dismissed from all future ministries. While this strategy was not implemented, there can be, no doubt, that Divine judgment was evident.

CHAPTER 14

REDEMPTIVE CONSCIOUSNESS

During this phase of the journey, we learned a lot about faith. While faith is our contractual relationship with God, it also works by doubt. That is, a certain degree of unbelief is required for belief. If I came to God, I must believe that He is God, and I must deny or disbelieve any pretender. If the Lord gave a promise, then all contradictions to that promise must be dismissed. While faith does not deny the reality of the contradictions, it does recognize that God has the last word in every situation. For by faith, we had to look beyond the obvious. We were not in denial of the truthfulness of the accusations, but there had been no word of the Lord regarding the future. So in the midst of a frenzy of predictions and public opinions, whose reports were we to believe? Well, we desperately needed a truthful strategy to navigate through this crisis in our own minds.

One of the messages that I preached during this latter phase of the scandal was titled *A Redemptive Consciousness*. It focused on the attention of the congregation upon their history with the Lord and addressed some of the ways they were managing the distress in their minds. By this time, a congregation of over 12,000 members had been reduced to about 1,500. Even though there were new members who had no history of the early years of the ministry, the majority of those who remained had been a part of the work from the opening of the Cathedral. The spiritual climate was, no doubt, greatly challenged and the memories of the former days lingered in the minds of many. I could very easily remember looking out over that vast congregation that once filled all of those burgundy padded pews. I could also remember the struggle to accommodate the influx of cars as people eagerly rushed to enter the building. Now, it was easily managed because there were many spaces to spare. The leaders and the people needed a Spirit directed strategy to navigate through a sea of doubt, anxiety, regret, and uncertainty.

A redemptive consciousness is an awareness of Divine purposes, priorities, and perspectives. It is the use of words, ideas, thoughts, and memories that enabled us to develop hope in the future and to be aware that God was working with us. Because my role on Sunday was to lead the congregation in prayer, I had access to the entire church. I constantly sought the Lord, along with others, for thoughts, ideas, words, and songs that focused the attention of the people upon the promises and work of the Lord and the needs of the people during the corporate prayer. I would lead the congregation in songs of hope and search for words to express the impressions in my heart. I always sensed the enabling of the Spirit during those times when the spiritual atmosphere was so thick with hopelessness and despair that it could be cut with a knife. There were times when I felt like a minority voice speaking against a majority opposition. Then I realized I was not alone, for there were many who embraced the idea of change. There was never any fear, dread, regret, nor anxiety within us.

I knew that the character of faith depended upon the quality of the message preached and believed. Also I strongly believed that the foundation of my messages were both Biblically and spiritually correct. I knew the difference between empty optimism and presumption. False hope is as dangerous as real fear. I was assured that the propositions set before the entire church were conditional. Repentance was needed, and people needed to stay aboard the ship. I readily accepted the reality that many of the people and leaders had a right to move on with their lives and ministries. In fact, Sandra and I counseled a number of individuals in such matters. Nevertheless, there had not been a definitive word from the Lord regarding the finality of the work. All I knew was simply the hope that the Spirit of God stirred within my heart.

The revelation of a redemptive consciousness enabled me to present my thoughts in a practical manner. First, I presented a full counsel perspective that kept us from vacillating back and forth between options, choices, opinions, and interests. There had to be an awareness of human opinions and Divine revelation. In fact, the judgment, mercy, and grace of God had to be kept in proper context. Grace is when we receive what we do not deserve, while mercy is when we do not receive the sentence for our mistakes. Judgment is never without mercy and grace. Second, I set forth an endurance perspective that sought to remind us all of an unfinished course and that there would be no failure if we did not quit. On many occasion, I would address the entire staff and declare that there was work to be done. In essence, there were unfulfilled prophecies that remained. And third, I labored to promote a foundation perspective that kept us conscious of the longevity and Biblical strength of this ministry.

This redemptive consciousness rested upon prophetic promises set before us from visiting ministers and from our own local presbyters that precipitated some hope in the future. A powerful incentive for endurance came from Job 14:7-9:

> *For there is hope of a tree, if it be cut down, that it will sprout again, and that the tender branch thereof will not cease. Though the root thereof wax old in the earth and the stock thereof die in the ground, yet through the scent of water it will bud and bring forth boughs like a plant.*

The prophetic language was so descriptive of the Cathedral because its beginning was likened to a twig becoming a great tree (Ezek. 17:22-24). Now this tree was cut down and had lost its credibility and life. The question was simple: Could credibility and productivity be restored?

There was also another prophetic reference taken from Psalms 126:

> *When the Lord turned again the captivity of Zion, we were like them that dream. Then was our mouth filled with laughter, and our tongue with singing: then said they among the heathen, The Lord hath done great things for them. The Lord hath done great things for us; whereof we are glad. Turn again our captivity, O Lord, as the streams in the south. They that sow in tears shall reap in joy. He that goeth forth and*

weepeth, bearing precious seed, shall doubtless come
again with rejoicing, bringing his sheaves with him.

While this narrative spoke of the astonishing promise of the restoration of Israel from exile in Babylon, I perceived thoughts of recovery and restoration of this ministry. Interestingly, there was the fulfillment of these propositions during the entire 1990s, for after two significant periods of public scandals, the credibility and productivity was restored to this work. During each of those periods, the Lord spoke to me from the prophet Isaiah 37-41. This Biblical record described the people of God under siege because of their idolatry. King Hezekiah was sick and near death, and he prayed for Divine deliverance. The Lord spoke to the prophet and gave promises of Hezekiah's healing and some wonderful signs of recovery. First, the sun dial would go backwards by ten degree. Second, the people would be sustained by vegetables and fruit that grew in their fields. Third, after three years, the foundations of people and provisions that had sustained them for three years would be reinforced and restored to its vitality and growth.

I felt strongly that this related to the Cathedral. The idea of Hezekiah being healed and given fifteen more years of life was critical. Bishop Paulk was critically ill with a desperate prognosis. However, his life was extended, and like Hezekiah, he wrote songs in the night. The signs of the recovery were most evident, for after the scandals were publicized, thousands of people and some leaders left the ministry, and that devastated the resources of the ministry. Yet the sign was that the people and gifts that remained in the ministry would be sufficient for its survival.

The sun dial being turned backwards signaled the return of missed opportunities and recovery of some privileges. During this three-year cycle, several critical ministry functions such as our international ministry school were restored. Furthermore, several staff members who had left the ministry returned during the three-year cycle. At the end of the three-year period (1992-1995), there was the restoration of credibility, visibility, and productivity of the ministry.

Even though these periods were present, I knew that faith and repentance were inseparable (Acts 2:38). To turn to God without forsaking the practices that precipitated the crisis would ultimately end in hypocrisy and failure (2 Pet. 2:20-22). This was a critical lesson for me since at times, I felt that I had been mistaken in my proclamations. However, one day after working in my yard, I was impressed with a most interesting thought. The burden of prophetic fulfillment does not rest upon the shoulders of the messenger. All prophecies are conditional and depend upon the correct response of the recipients. Once the messenger delivers the word, there remains no responsibility for its fulfillment except upon those who receive or reject the word. This was a tremendous source of comfort to me, personally.

CHAPTER 15

DAILY CARE OF THE CHURCH

As previously noted, during our visit to other churches and ministries, we were constantly questioned about the status of the ministry and the people. Strangely, enough, there were obvious concerns about the state of the key leaders, however, but there were many questions and concerns about the congregation. The following questions were asked: Are the people leaving or staying? How are the people handling the crisis? What is it like to be in the midst of such a crisis? Since the ministry of the Cathedral was such a highly respectable model of a local church and many emulated its teachings and programs, I felt it necessary to respond to the many inquiries.

First of all, something needs to be said about the atmosphere at the Cathedral during a crisis of such magnitude. With such allegations of sexual immorality against key leaders, the people were definitely in a state of shock. Emotional responses ranged from disbelief, denial, sadness, fear, disillusionment, despair, disrespect, anger, resentment, bitterness, and even rage. Some members even questioned their own faith and beliefs while others simply contemplated their future association with the ministry. The public media, and even the religious community, presented their own personal commentaries on the nature and implications of the crisis. The accusations against a few precipitated an assault against the entire church. The crisis attracted the attention of major news publications and broadcasts, especially religious programs. Occult, false doctrine, heresies, abuse, toxic faith, and spiritual deception were among the allegations levied against the entire ministry. There were also other concerns: Were the reports true? How could this happen? Are other people involved? Family members of many congregants who were not members of the church were in distress and expressed grave concern for their relatives who remained a part of the church.

During the crisis, there was still a need to minister life and hope to people, visit the sick, arrange funerals, plan weddings, and provide counsel for members. In essence, there were efforts to maintain some degree of normalcy in the midst of the most challenging environment. When the congregation had been over 12,000 people, they had been divided into twelve pastoral groups. An elder and a host of deacons and caregivers managed each group. Although these elders met regularly with their members, the nature of these meetings were now conditioned by the crisis, including people leaving. There were questions that demanded specific answers. At times, fear, confusion, anger, frustration, resentment, and even bitterness surfaced among the people. Factions were developed among the congregation based upon the belief or disbelief of the accusations. Longstanding friendships were challenged and, at times, even disrupted based upon the acceptance or rejections of the reports. Suspicions and accusations were directed toward all of the elders.

During such times, the elders sought to give answers to critical questions. First of all, this was not simply spiritual warfare that was to be managed by prayer, fasting, and long vigils of denunciation of demonic powers. Secondly, this was not the chastening of the Lord to remove some of the leaders and people who subsequently left the church. Thirdly, the crisis was not some spiritual test to determine the level of faith and dedication of church. And finally, since the accusations had not yet been proven, it was not profitable to disrupt the entire ministry.

As leaders, we sought to set everything in a proper perspective. The crisis did not involve the entire leadership and neither was the crisis rampant throughout the entire church. Such human failure did not incriminate God. Even though God is sovereign and knows all things, there is still the right of human free will. Therefore, regardless of the accusations, we believed that the crisis should not shatter faith in God nor raise suspicion and even disdain for such Biblical concepts as holiness, submission, authority, sowing, reaping, faith, and Kingdom of God.

Since the accusations involved the alleged abuse of women and inappropriate use of authority and submission, the theology and doctrine of the entire ministry came under scrutiny. This was a major issue among other leaders and pastors of churches. They desired to know if the accusations were true, was there a supporting theology to justify such behavior? Can individuals reach a level of faith that allows them freedom that is denied for others? Are there "sins of the flesh and sins of the spirit?" As leaders, we worked diligently to shepherd the people. A few leaders among us were defensive and sought to denounce the accusations, while others sought to examine the truthfulness of the reports. Some leaders left the ministry because of personal convictions. Interestingly enough, the crisis precipitated the departure of some leaders to begin their own ministry. Although the precipitating factors may have been unfortunate, the new ministries that sprang up would prove to be a blessing in the economy of God.

As earlier stated, a Divine perspective was absolutely necessary. In the midst of a frenzy of public opinions, there was a constant need for proper discernment. Because the people and leaders who remained in the ministry were thought to be in agreement with the nature of the transgression or in denial of the reality of the problems, the relational integrity of the ministry had to be addressed. Was it possible to remain in the ministry without being in agreement with the beliefs that precipitated the crisis? Can two walk together unless they agree? Does association with a group always mean identification with the beliefs of that group? Personally, I believe that there can be presence without participation. That is, it was possible to be members of the Cathedral without endorsing the mistakes at hand or even denying their existence. We stressed this principle of association without identification regularly.

As we have noted throughout this narrative, we sought Biblical models and examples to substantiate what we were sensing in our hearts. During the services and the gathering of the presbytery, I would set forth the proposition that we should "pray and stay." Each pastor searched his/her own heart concerning the issues at hand. Many of the leaders and members of the congregation had been associated with the ministry for twenty to thirty years. Some had even been a part of the ministry since its very beginning in Atlanta. A large number of the congregation had worshipped together in the first constructed building on the newly acquired property in Decatur, Georgia. In fact, many of us had shared a winter and summer together in a large tent that served as a temporary housing for the ministry while a new construction was underway. As a worshipping community, we had labored together to build a transitional building called the K-Center, which resembled a gigantic airplane garage. That same building had accommodated the huge crowds and representatives from over eighty nations who gathered for the first conference on the *Kingdom of God* in 1990. The majority of the leaders and people had witnessed the construction of an adjacent building called the Atrium. It was completed "without sweat," according to the words of the notable Archbishop Benson Idahosa, the apostle from Africa. This congregation of people had been a part of a crowd of over 12,000 that filled the newly constructed Cathedral to capacity on its opening day. So, there was a common history and strong interpersonal bonds that kept the congregation together for a while.

As the head of the network of churches associated with the Cathedral, my role was to travel and minister in the various churches. As mentioned before, there were many questions and concerns among the 200 churches and ministries that were a part of the network. While some of them severed their relationships with us, many remained a part of the network. A frequently asked question was why the leaders and the people remained members of the Cathedral. Again, although there was a common history, there was also a conviction that the Lord had brought us all together from the beginning. Furthermore, there had not been a Divine mandate for us to abandon the work.

Interestingly, enough, the crisis at the Cathedral precipitated a prophetic frenzy both without and within the redeemed community. There were predictions regarding the future of the entire ministry. There were even proclamations of the judgment of death for those directly involved with the crisis and even upon all those who remained with the ministry. A critical question in the entire process was discerning the Divine judgment: Was there a Divine plan for the recovery of those central to the crisis and the ministry? Was there a future for the entire ministry of the Cathedral? If so, what would be the strategy used to accomplish this plan?

Prophecy proved to be most valuable solution during the cycle of the crisis. Prophecy is a sign to believers (1 Cor. 14:22). It is most valuable for the edification, exhortation and comfort of the saints (1 Cor. 14:3). However, prophecy must be discerned (1 Cor. 14:29) for its source (Divine, human, or demonic), content (message communicated) and intent (expected human response). Prophecy should not violate the character of God or the integrity of Scripture. During the crisis, there were prophetic decrees and promises that offered hope for the future. There was a primary concern, though, for there was no public recognition of responsibility; for that reason, the management of the crisis was viewed as a denial of reality and an exoneration of any guilt. In this next section, we will examine the role of prophets and prophecy during the crisis.

CHAPTER 16

PROPHETS AND PROPHECY

Personal prophecy has been a constant companion of Sandra and mine during this journey. Of course, we have personally witnessed it as an indispensable tool of encouragement, counsel, direction, and even correction. It has never been a substitute for the Scripture, but it has been a testimony of God's sovereignty where He often declares the ending of a situation from the beginning. This, we discovered, is the "mystery of prophecy" in which promises are made or direction is given, but details and process of fulfillment would be lacking. In retrospect, this is so true since at the very beginning of our journey, prophetic predictions and decrees were given regarding our personal life and ministry. Nevertheless, there was no information regarding the people, experiences, and events that would be a vital part of the fulfillment of those promises. Prophecy has always stimulated a consciousness of God; stirred faith in our hearts; and reminded us of Divine involvement in our lives.

Prophecy is always a mixture of the human and the Divine and must be judged for its source (Divine, human, demonic), content (words, language, message), and intent (encouragement, correction, instruction). Prophetic words will also contain an expression of the messenger's personal doctrine and convictions because messengers are human vessels and limited by their own knowledge, revelation and linguistic preferences (Jer. 28; 2 Pet. 2:1; 1 John 4:1; Rev. 19:20). Thus, God will speak, but often what He says and means is affected by the speaker's limitation. This we found to be true, when some of the visiting ministers came to the Cathedral with words that focused upon spiritual authority, warfare, and anointing. While many prophetic assessments of the crisis and its resolution were most beneficial and accurate, there were also the presence of personal opinions and conviction expressed in some of the utterances. The need to discern God's meaning within the utterance became paramount.

Thus, we can herein recognize that prophecy often frustrates the church since it declares the end from the beginning but rarely reveals the middle part. The middle part relates to the process of fulfillment. As previously stated, this is the "mystery of prophecy," for its words not only reveal information but they also conceal details. This mystery often creates the "crisis of prophecy," for often, there is a disparity between what is anticipated and what is ultimately realized. For example, during the early phases of the crisis, there were prophetic words that spoke of the restoration of the visibility, credibility, and productivity of this ministry. We thought this meant happy and productive times and the coming of many people. Indeed, people did come, but they came out of curiosity rather than coming to be part of the work. Part of the visibility came when the news media converged upon us with their cameras and pens and made the scandal a national and international story. I discovered that before credibility comes, there would come a period incredibility. Also, before productivity arrives, there would be times of non-productivity. While we were looking for immediate periods of positive events, we, instead, experienced some very challenging ones.

We discovered that the most significant aspect of personal prophecy is it conditionality. That is, Divine promises and predictions are dependent upon the response of the recipients. This was very frustrating, to me, during the journey since there were wonderful promises and predictions regarding the future of this ministry. I spoke many of them, and I knew that the condition was repentance. While no one is exempt from the need of repentance, the issues and the individuals involved in the scandal were specific. Repentance is both conceptual and behavioral: in other words, it requires both change in belief and understanding with a complete reformation in personal behavior or action.

The memories of those prophetic moments are still vivid in my mind, today. I often wondered: Were my words clear enough? Was there some deficiency on my part? Was I bold enough to say all that was impressed upon my heart? After all, to make announcements of the coming of recovery and restoration were bold statements on my part. Still, my greatest frustration was not seeing those events come to pass as I envisioned them. I, no doubt, struggled in my own mind. Was I wrong? Were these simply my own hopes and aspirations for the ministry? Was I in denial of reality of the conditions that were present? Was I generating false hopes? Those "prophetic contradictions" were constant companions in my mind, but I would not deny what I perceived of the Lord.

Again, one day during a time of reflection, a thought came

to my mind, and that was a source of great comfort to me. I was impressed with the thought that the fulfillment of prophetic words does not rest upon the shoulders of the messenger but upon the recipients. I had assumed some degree of responsibility for the lack of fulfillment. My emotional pain was constant. Although I knew that there were phases of the ministry that were completed, there was still so much more to be done. I was not in denial of reality, but I was recognizing finality. The scandals were never imaginary in my mind, nor was I in disbelief of all the accusations. However, there were Divine promises. In fact, this taught me that faith is not the denial of reality: rather, it is the recognition of God's finality. I firmly believe that God has the last word in every situation. However, there is also the issue of free will and human response.

Since the initial crisis in 1990 and the subsequent accusations over the next fifteen years had affected the size of the congregation, financial support, and the outreach capability of the ministry, as previously mentioned, there were prophecies regarding the restoration of the credibility, visibility and profitability of the ministry. There were years of recovery and restoration that followed the initial crisis of 1990. While all of the accusations were never absolutely proven, there remained clouds of suspicion, doubt, distrust, and dissension. It became increasingly obvious that the credibility of some of the accusations could not be so easily dismissed. The last crisis which erupted in 2003, involved some very public and credible people. This crisis received tremendous legal and public treatment. The accusations could not be denied nor could those who brought the accusation be discredited.

From 2003 until the selling of the Cathedral property, there were internal events that signaled the end of a phase of the ministry and the beginning of a new phase. First, there was the declining health of Archbishop Paulk that greatly diminished his capacity to lead the church. Second, there was the transfer of the leadership of the ministry and the introduction of new ideas and practices. Third, there was the continued loss of financial support due to a dwindling congregation. All of these signs signaled the end of the work at its present location. The property was sold in 2009, and the small congregation relocated.

In retrospect, it could be argued that prophecy that is not fulfilled is false. A strong case could also be made against the objectivity of the prophet who seeks to speak about the community where he works. A case could also be made that this prophet stayed in the ministry too long. In response to these possibilities, it should be noted that no Biblical precedent exists where the Lord removed prophetic voices from His people when they were in distress or rebellion. Furthermore, prophecy is always to be judged for its content, intent, and source. I did not waver in my conviction even though certain phases of the ministry had been fulfilled, and there were certain aspects of the work that were yet to be done. For those reasons and in obedience to the Lord, I never anticipated leaving the work until the Lord released me. That release came at the death of Archbishop Paulk, the selling of the property, and the movement of the ministry in another direction.

CHAPTER 17

REFLECTIONS

While navigating this journey that began thirty years ago, Sandra and I have learned a lot. At the beginning, we received landmarks that helped us along the way, and they came in the form of admonitions. Also, we were to endure difficult challenges and not become entangled nor overwhelmed by them (2 Tim. 2:3-4). We were given spiritual gifts that enabled us to provide wisdom, counsel, and direction to people (Luke 4:18; Tit. 1:5; Prov. 23:19-21). Along the way, we were most fortunate to learn much about the ways of the Lord and the Divine/human connection that started all of the visions, dreams, and ministries. Some are encapsulated in the following proverbial statements:

*Prayer and prophetic utterance reveal our concepts of God.

*The ways of the Lord breed confusion among those who are only accustomed to His acts.

*The Lord loves mercy and not sacrifice, and He offers life after sin when there is repentance.

*The Lord distinguishes between rebellion, ignorance, maturity, and immaturity.

*Gifts and callings may take you to the top of the mountain but only integrity will keep you there.

*Gifts and callings should be sanctified, but there are times when they are not.

*Because a divine sentence against an evil work is not executed speedily, they that perform the work become more entrenched in it, and the grace of God is often mistaken as tolerance.

*Desperation is the catalyst for irrationality. Poor judgment is often precipitated by moments of desperation.

*When people lose consciousness of the Lord, it becomes evident in their behavior, attitude, and lifestyles.

*The Lord changes history when He grants a different perspective of past events.

*People can prophesy out of their doctrine and convictions.

*The crisis of prophecy is the difference between what is anticipated and what is finally realized.

*The mystery of prophecy is not what it reveals but what it conceals.

*Prophecy frustrates the church because it declares the end from the beginning, and it omits the middle details or the process.

*Human addiction can be non-chemical, social, theological, and behavioral; there can be addiction to a person, place, status, time, and even a truth.

*Spiritual warfare is not what we do on our knees but what we do on our feet and in our minds.

*In a multitude of counsel, there is both safety and danger… a lot of people can be wrong.

*Longevity, popularity, and sincerity are not always criteria of truth.

*When telling the truth becomes a liability, then there is no truth shared.

*Counselors are both a tremendous source of strength and weakness in a ministry. They must know what to reveal to leaders and what to conceal.

It should be noted that there were no enemies in these crises, but there were estranged friends. Therefore, no one was to be labeled as the agent of the devil. Everyone was of God, but each was hurt, wounded, disillusioned, confused, and frustrated over the events that occurred.

The honest truth regarding the causes, effects, and ultimate implications of the "precipitating events" surrounding the life and ministry of the Chapel Hill Harvester Church/Cathedral of the Holy Spirit and its key leadership may never be fully known. There are some memories that will never fade, and there are some pains that will never go away. Additionally, public opinions will surface whenever this ministry is discussed. As a result, some will attempt to discount the entire life and legacy of the work and its primary leader, Archbishop Earl Paulk. Others may even seek to diminish the accusations, mistakes, and failures and simply magnify the accomplishments of the entire work. Some may even raise suspicion and skepticism regarding Charismatic and Pentecostal Christians who profess to hear from God and respond to visions, prophecies, and revelations. This latter possibility is surely to come since many works have been written as a critique of previous times of revival or reformation emphasis such as Word of Faith, Prophetic Ministry, and Shepherding. Finally, there may be efforts to slander the entire Cathedral experience simply because it falls outside of the boundaries of certain spiritual and theological borders. Regardless of the response to the history of this work, however, the accomplishments of the leaders and the people cannot be diminished nor discredited. With the passing of time, the names and faces of those individuals who were so publicized in the media during the height of the scandals may be forgotten. For those who were a part of this journey, however, the memories will remain. Should there be any future literary treatment of the legacy of Chapel Hill Harvester/Cathedral of the Holy Spirit, a fair assessment should conclude that it was a God-ordained story and not simply a chronicle of human mistakes and failures.

The critical questions still remain: Did the ministry end tragically, or did the ministry finish its course? Why did Sandra and I remain a part of the work until the very end? In my opinion, the work finished its course in the following ways:

*as an agent of proclamation and demonstration of the principles and power of the Kingdom of God at a local church level

*mobilization of the saints in ministry

*construction of a neo-gothic Cathedral as visible expression of the connection between theology and structure

*the introduction of innovative evangelism through expressive worship, arts and education

*demonstration of the co-existence of form and power in liturgy

*demonstration of strategies for the recovery and restoration of the fallen

*reconciliation of racial and cultural divisions

*initiation of a convergence of denominational factions

*integration of office of bishop into the Charismatic/Pentecostal dimensions.

The Chapel Hill Harvester Church/Cathedral of the Holy Spirit, as a distinct entity, is now represented in many different factions and expressions among individuals and corporate groups, ministries and churches. Archbishop Earl Paulk finished his course in the most critical phase of his ministry as a provoker of change through the proclamation and demonstration of historic ideas, thoughts, practices and traditions that precipitated revival in the interest of the Kingdom of God and the name of Jesus. His leadership, along with others, inaugurated the idea of mega church during the 1980s and spearheaded a dialogue between the Roman Catholic Church and the Pentecostal Churches through The International Communion of Charismatic Churches. There were, in my judgment, years left for him to still be a productive resource of revelation, counsel, knowledge and wisdom to a generation at hand and the one to come.

The final question remains to be answered. Why did Sandra and I remain associated with the ministry until the very end? In fact, I preached one of the last messages in the Cathedral two weeks before it was sold. Indeed, after thirty years of ministry, we had witnessed every major transition of this work. There were many glorious moments, and there were times when we despaired over life itself. Major prophets prophesied that if we stayed in the ministry too long or did not leave, our credibility and integrity would be questioned. Indeed, this happened since many of our personal ministry associations and alliances were discontinued. However, we are also quick to say that many ministerial relationships remained and increased. Other notable leaders even claimed that we were too loyal to people. One individual noted, "Even rats get off a sinking ship." Even some of our family members and friends questioned our continued association with the ministry. While they all had a right to their opinions, we felt they were searching for an understanding of the nature and scope of such a crisis. While many of those inquiries did trouble us, we knew that our commitment was to God and not to a ministry or an individual. We had no choice but to willingly obey since our confidence and assurance in life rest upon His grace and our obedience to His will.

Sandra and I often discussed these issues between ourselves. Nevertheless, obedience to the Lord was more important than anything. The Spirit never commissioned us to leave. At the height of the crisis, however, I was impressed with the narrative recorded in Jeremiah 15. The prophet lamented over his status, which could have been a physical matter or a spiritual conflict. Nevertheless, the Lord did not answer his inquiry directly. Instead, the Spirit set forth a proposition that if Jeremiah would take the precious from the vile and maintained his position among the people, he would be a voice for the Lord. He was instructed not to go with the people but the people could come to him. This narrative was very helpful and promising to us, for we felt that the Lord had directed us to this ministry, so He would direct us in this crisis.

There were also other prophetic words, which came from notable prophets. They identified us as stewards who would take the old and new and preserve that which is precious to the Lord. One prophecy stressed the idea that our work would not depend upon financiers and that the Lord had enlarged our vision and the dimensions of our ministry. In fact, I was impressed with some wonderful thoughts during my very last visit to the Cathedral property on March 12, 2009. It was an early morning, and my pattern at that time was to jog around all of the Cathedral property. On this particular morning, I made my last visit to the Presbytery room on the second floor of the Garlington Mall. I had spent many years in meetings there with my fellow elders. It was there, where we had sought the Lord and prayed over matters of the church. During a few moments that morning, I was overwhelmed by the presence of the Holy Spirit. While my heart was saddened by the memories, and tears moistened my face, I found a piece of paper and a pen in one of the desk drawers and fervently began to write the impressions that filled my mind. This phase of our lives and ministry was over and a new phase had begun. I would perform the things that the Lord had spoken through me for this Cathedral ministry in another place. The new work would spring up like a tree in a desert, and it would bear fruit overnight. Not a word spoken nor a promise or decree made would go unnoticed. Wisdom and knowledge will prevail. Our household will be stewards of His truths. For the Lord would raise up His cause without struggle. I was commanded not to weep anymore for this work.

We simply stayed because it was the will of the Lord. We are neither to be complimented nor assigned some badge of valor. Instead, we, along with many others, simply recognized the sovereignty of God. This was and still remains His ministry. The remaining congregation of people and leaders have moved on with their lives and ministries. Sandra and I have begun a local church. Meanwhile, we continue to write books and oversee churches and ministries both nationally and internationally. We still maintain our private practice of dentistry located a short walking distance from our home and the main Cathedral sanctuary. A growing and exciting Baptist congregation now occupies the Cathedral building.

It is tragic that the "precipitating factors" of moral and ethical allegations seemed to have commanded more attention than the aforementioned accomplishments. Nevertheless, the achievements of this ministry, under the leadership of Archbishop Paulk and the many elders, cannot be ignored nor forgotten. My last conversation with him a few days before he passed away revealed the passion he still had in his heart for the Kingdom of God and the Church. The fact that he passed away under such circumstances was tragic to his family, friends, the Cathedral, and, to me, personally.

We stand indebted to God for the privilege to have experienced such a ministry with all of its leaders and people. We have no regrets because of our association with this ministry. However, we remain very sad for the many people who were wounded, abandoned or estranged in any way. We know that some memories will neither fade nor be wasted. When history is a teacher, then the future becomes a friend. The footprints of Chapel Hill Harvester/Cathedral of the Holy Spirit will remain, but it must be remembered that forgiveness is not memory loss, but, rather, it is memory without vengeance.

Endnotes

1. Earl Paulk, *20/20 Vision: A Clear View of the Kingdom of God*, Atlanta: Kingdom Publishers, 1988.

2. Earl Paulk, *The Ultimate Kingdom: Lessons for Today's Christian From the Book of Revelation*, Atlanta: K Dimension Publishers, 1986.

3. Earl Paulk, *Held in the Heavens Until: God's Strategy For Planet Earth*, Atlanta: K Dimension Publishers, 1985.

4. Earl Paulk, *The Prophetic Community: God Answers the Prayer of His Son*, Shippensburg, Pa.: Destiny Image Publishers, 1995.

5. Earl Paulk, *The Local Church Says Hell, No!: The Vision of One Congregation Fighting the Enemy In His Own Backyard*, Atlanta: Kingdom Publishers, 1991.

6. Earl Paulk, *The Great Escape Theory*, Decatur, Georgia: Chapel Hill Harvester Church, 1988.

7. Earl Paulk and Daniel Rhodes, *A Theology for the News Millennium*, Atlanta, Ga: Earl Paulk Ministries, 2000.

8. Kirby Clements, *A Philosophy of Ministry*, Decatur, Ga: Clements Family Ministry, 1995.

9. Bruce Barron, *The Charismatics Path to South African Brotherhood*, New York: Wall Street Journal, 1987.

[10] *Unity and Diversity in the New Testament,* op. cit., p.351-362.

[11] Ronald A. N. Kydd, *Charismatic Gifts in the Early Church: An Exploration Into the Gifts of the Spirit During the First Three Centuries of the Christian Church,* Peabody, Ma.: Hendrickson Publishers, 1984.

[12] William J. Bausch, *Pilgrim Church: A Popular History of Catholic Christianity,* Mystic, Conn.: Twenty-Third Publications, 1989.

[13] Robert Webber, *Worship: Old and New*, Grand Rapids: Zondervan, 1992.

[14] Kirby Clements, *A Philosophy of Ministry*, Decatur, Ga: Clements Family Ministries 1993.

CPSIA information can be obtained at www.ICGtesting.com
Printed in the USA
LVOW01s1309140815

450133LV00001B/1/P